Teaching
Film and TV
Documentary

Sarah Casey Benyahia

Series Editor: Vivienne Clark
Commissioning Editor: Wendy Earle

British Library Cataloguing-in-Publication Data
A catalogue record for this guide is available from the British Library

ISBN 978-1-84457-223-6

First published in 2007 by the British Film Institute
21 Stephen Street, London W1T 1LN

Student worksheets to support this guide are supplied at: www.bfi.org.uk/tfms
User name: **docs@bfi.org.uk** Password: **te1612do**

Design: Amanda Hawkes
Cover photograph: *Être et Avoir*, courtesy of BFI Stills
Printed in Great Britain by: Cromwell Press Ltd

www.bfi.org.uk
There's more to discover about film and television through the BFI.
Our world-renowned archive, cinemas, festivals, films, publications
and learning resources are here to inspire you.

Contents

Introduction to the series   1

1 Introduction   5
Assessment contexts   5
Approaches to teaching   7
How to use this guide   13
Scheme of work 1: Documentary realism and representation   14
Scheme of work 2: Documentary, propaganda and persuasion   15

2 Background   17
Approaches to documentary   17
Documentary realism and representation   22
Modes of documentary   29

3 Case studies   36
Case study 1: Documentary, propaganda and social and political change   36
Case study 2: Observational documentary and the new television formats   54
Case study 3: Documentary and performance   73

Glossary   95
References and resources   99
Bibliography   99
Filmography   100
Useful websites   105
Acknowledgements   106

Introduction to the series

Since the introduction of the revised post-16 qualifications (AS and A2 Level) in the UK in September 2000, the number of students taking A Level Film and Media Studies has increased significantly, a trend shown by the latest entry statistics.

Subject & Level	June 2001	June 2002	June 2005	June 2006
A Level Film Studies+	2017	–	–	–
AS Level Film Studies	3852	–	9188	9703
A2 Level Film Studies	–	2175	4913	5898
A Level Media Studies*+	16,293	–	–	–
AS Level Media Studies*	22,872	–	32,346	33,542
A2 Level Media Studies*	–	18,150	23,427	25,192

*Three combined awarding bodies' results
+Legacy syllabus – last entry June 2001
(Source: BFI Education website – AS/A2 statistics refer to cashed-in entries only)

Furthermore, changes to the 14–19 curriculum currently in development for 2008 will doubtless see further increases in the take-up of courses (and indeed new courses) in this popular subject area. In response to this continuing expansion (unabated despite criticism from ill-informed pundits), a professional association of media educators in the UK (MEA – www.mediaedassociation.org.uk) has been formed to support teachers at all levels in all learning contexts, as well as to provide much-needed accurate public relations information and guidance about the many courses on offer and how to differentiate between them.

Inevitably these increases in student numbers have led to a pressing demand for more teachers and both new and experienced teachers (from other disciplines) alike may be faced with teaching these subjects for the first time, without necessarily a degree-level background to help them with subject content and conceptual understanding. In addition, frequently changing specifications see the arrival of new set topics and areas of study, so there is a continued need for up-to-date resources to aid teacher preparation. Media study is most effective when it responds to current media output and issues and it is the aim of this series to provide reference to recent media texts and products as well as to older ones.

I developed the concept and format of this series with the above factors, and busy and enthusiastic teachers and creative and energetic students, in mind. Each title provides an accessible reference resource, with essential topic content, as well as clear guidance on good classroom practice to improve the quality of teaching and students' learning. We are confident that, as well as supporting the teacher new to these subjects, the series provides the experienced specialist with new critical perspectives and teaching approaches as well as useful content.

The two sample schemes of work included in Section 1 are intended as practical models to help get teachers started. They are not prescriptive, as any effective scheme of work has to be developed with the specific requirements of an assessment context, and the ability of the teaching group, in mind. Likewise, the worksheets provided in the online materials offer examples of good practice, which can be adapted to specific needs and contexts. In some cases, the online provision includes additional resources, such as interviews and illustrative material, available as webnotes. See www.bfi.org.uk/tfms.

The series is clear evidence of the range, depth and breadth of teacher expertise and specialist knowledge required at A Level in these subjects. Also, it is an affirmation of why this subject area is such an important, rich and compelling one for increasing numbers of 16- to 19-year-old students. Many of the more theoretical titles in the series include reference to practical exercises involving media production skills. It is important that it is understood here that the current A Levels in Media and Film Studies are not designed as vocational, or pre-vocational, qualifications. In these contexts, the place of practical media production is to offer students active, creative and engaging ways in which to explore theory and reflect on their own practice.

It has been very gratifying to see that several titles in this series have found an international audience, in the USA, Canada and Australia, among other countries, and we hope that future titles continue to be of interest in international moving image education. Every author in the series is an experienced teacher of Film and/or Media Studies at this level and many have examining/moderating experience. It has been a pleasure to work so closely with such a diverse range of committed professionals and I should like to thank them for their individual contributions to this expanding series.

Vivienne Clark
Series Editor
January 2007

● Key features

- Assessment contexts for the major UK post-16 Film and Media Studies specifications
- Suggested schemes of work
- Historical contexts (where appropriate)
- Key facts, statistics and terms
- Detailed reference to the key concepts of Film and Media Studies
- Detailed case studies
- Glossaries
- Bibliographies
- Student worksheets, activities and resources (available online) – ready to print and photocopy for the classroom.

● Other titles available in the series include:

- *Teaching Scriptwriting, Screenplays and Storyboards for Film and TV Production* (Mark Readman);
- *Teaching TV Sitcom* (James Baker);
- *Teaching Digital Video Production* (Pete Fraser and Barney Oram);
- *Teaching TV News* (Eileen Lewis);
- *Teaching Women and Film* (Sarah Gilligan);
- *Teaching World Cinema* (Kate Gamm);
- *Teaching TV Soaps* (Lou Alexander and Alison Cousens);
- *Teaching Contemporary British Broadcasting* (Rachel Viney);
- *Teaching Contemporary British Cinema* (Sarah Casey Benyahia);
- *Teaching Music Video* (Pete Fraser);
- *Teaching Auteur Study* (David Wharton and Jeremy Grant);
- *Teaching Analysis of Film Language* (David Wharton and Jeremy Grant);
- *Teaching Men and Film* (Matthew Hall);
- *Teaching Film Censorship and Controversy* (Mark Readman);
- *Teaching Stars and Performance* (Jill Poppy);
- *Teaching Video Games* (James Newman and Barney Oram);
- *Teaching Black Cinema* (Peter Jones).

● Forthcoming titles include:

Teaching TV Drama and *Teaching Short Films*.

SERIES EDITOR: Vivienne Clark is a teacher of Film and Media Studies at Langley Park School for Boys, Beckenham, Kent. She is currently an Associate Tutor of BFI Education and formerly a Principal Examiner for A Level Media Studies for one of the English awarding bodies. She is also a freelance teacher trainer, media education consultant and writer/editor, with several published textbooks and resources, including *GCSE Media Studies* (Longman 2002), *Key Concepts and Skills for Media Studies* (Hodder Arnold 2002) and *The Complete A–Z Film and Media Studies Handbook* (Hodder & Stoughton 2007). She is also a course tutor for the BFI/Institute of Education MA module, An Introduction to Media Education Practice.

AUTHOR:

Sarah Casey Benyahia is currently a teacher of Film and Media studies at Colchester Sixth Form College and has experience of teaching on a range of Further and Higher Education courses at A Level, BTEC and degree level. She was formerly a Principal Examiner for one of the English awarding bodies and is the author of *Teaching Contemporary British Cinema* (BFI 2005).

Introduction

Assessment contexts

Awarding body & level	Subject	Unit code	Module/Topic
✓ AQA AS Level	Media Studies	Med 1	Reading the Media
		Med 2	Textual Topics: Documentary
✓ AQA A2 Level	Media Studies	Med 6	Comparative Critical Analysis
✓ Edexcel BTEC National Diploma	Media Studies		Understanding the Media
✓ EdExcel BTEC National Diploma	Media Studies		Television and Video Studies
✓ OCR AS Level	Media Studies	2731	Textual Analysis
✓ OCR AS Level	Media Studies	2732	Audience and Institutions
✓ OCR A2 Level	Media Studies	2735	Media Issues and Debates: Topic: Contemporary British Broadcasting
✓ WJEC AS Level	Film Studies	FS3	Messages and Values: Social and Political Conflict: Focus film: *Bloody Sunday*
✓ WJEC A2 Level	Film Studies	FS6	Critical Studies: Section A: Documentary
✓ SQA Higher	Media Studies	D332	12 Media Analysis
✓ SQA Advanced Higher	Media Studies	D332	13 Media Analysis
✓ SQA Advanced Higher	Media Studies	DF15	12 Media Analysis: Non-fiction: Television and Film Documentary
✓ CCEA AS Level	Moving Image Arts	AS2	Critical Response
✓ CCEA A2 Level	Moving Image Arts	A21	Creative Production and Research
✓ CCEA A2 Level	Moving Image Arts	A22	Critical Response and Specialisation

Other titles in this series offer excellent complementary information to this guide:
- *Teaching Analysis of Film Language* – David Wharton and Jeremy Grant
- *Teaching Contemporary British Broadcasting* – Rachel Viney
- *Teaching Contemporary British Cinema* – Sarah Casey Benyahia.

● Specification links

The study of film and television documentary is appropriate to the following specifications. The relevant areas of the units are listed below, with a direct link to the section in the guide provided where necessary.

AQA AS Level Media Studies – Med 1: Reading the Media, AQA A2 Level Media Studies – Med 6: Comparative Critical Analysis

- Knowledge and application of key concepts; media language, representation, values and ideology, institutions.
- Textual analysis of unseen media texts.

AQA AS Level Media Studies – Med 2: Textual Topics: Documentary

- Close study of a range of documentary texts (including pre-1990).
- Study of audience and institutional contexts.
- The case studies can be used as the basis for study of this topic (Case study 1 deals with historical examples, Case study 2 includes work on popular factual television programming).

OCR AS Level Media Studies – Unit 2731: Textual Analysis

- Technical aspects of moving image (unseen analysis).

OCR AS Level Media Studies – Unit 2732: Audience and Institutions

- New media technologies and ownership.
- Case study 2 (Popular factual programming and convergence).

OCR A2 Level Media Studies – Unit 2735: Media Issues and Debates: Topic: Contemporary British Broadcasting

- Case study 2 (Docusoaps and reality television); Case study 3 (documentary-drama).

WJEC AS Level Film Studies – FS3: Messages and Values: Social and Political Conflict: Focus film: *Bloody Sunday*

- Case study 3 (documentary-drama).

WJEC A2 Level Film Studies – FS6: Critical Studies: Section A: Documentary

- Theories of realism and representation, range of textual studies.
- Section 2: Background, Case study 2 (Direct cinema); Case study 3 (Performative documentary).

SQA Higher Media Studies – D332 12: Media Analysis

- Analysis of a range of media texts including film.

SQA Advanced Higher Media Studies – D332 13: Media Analysis
- Economic, institutional, ideological contexts.
- Case study 1 (Propaganda); Case study 2 (Reality television and convergence).

SQA Advanced Higher Media Studies – DF15 12: Media Analysis: Non-Fiction: Television and Film Documentary

CCEA AS Level Moving Image Arts – AS2: Critical Response
- Unseen moving image text.

CCEA A2 Level Moving Image Arts – A21: Creative Production and Research
- Use of documentary techniques in film.

CCEA A2 Level Moving Image Arts – A22: Critical Response and Specialisation
- Unseen moving image text
- Specialist research – purpose and meaning of the work of historical or contemporary filmmaker.
- Case study 1 (John Grierson); Case study 3 (Nick Broomfield).

Approaches to teaching

• Why teach film and television documentary?
   A rationale for teachers

This topic provides the opportunity to explore all the key concepts in Film and Media Studies:

- Film and media language
The identification of different documentary techniques, defining documentary as a genre, distinguishing between the different documentary styles or modes. See Documentary realism and representation p22.

- Institutions
The way in which public service broadcasting and state funding of documentary in both historical and contemporary contexts affects the type of documentary produced. Also relevant is the use of documentary formats by satellite and digital television channels in developing audience share and interactive technologies. In addition to television documentary, the funding of documentary for cinema release raises questions of independent and indigenous film production in opposition to the dominance of Hollywood studios. See Case study 1 (British documentary movement) and Case study 2 (Convergence).

● Audiences

There is obviously a link between issues raised by institutional context and the concept of audience, eg the use of interactive technology and documentary formats to target a youth audience. In addition to audience segmentation, the processes of interpretation are central to the concept of propaganda and persuasion in documentary forms.

See Case study 1 and Case study 3.

● Representation

This is a central area of overlap with the analysis of fictional forms and again raises questions about the documentary's relationship to reality. The documentary represents people, places and ideas through similar techniques of construction and audience manipulation as those used by fiction films. See Background, Documentary realism and representation and Case study 1 (*Night Mail*); Case study 2 (*Être et Avoir*).

Representation in relation to documentary also refers to the concept of re-presenting the world, rather than directly reflecting reality.

● Messages and values; ideology

The study of documentary provides a variety of examples that reinforce or subvert dominant ideology and the values of society. This can be defined in an explicit way – the use of documentary as state propaganda – but also in more subtle ways through the representations of groups and places. See Case study 1.

Defining the documentary

As is evident in the more detailed theoretical discussion below (see p29), defining the documentary is complicated because of the many different forms and styles. The development of reality TV in particular has added to the debate about definitions of documentary. There are, though, some initial expectations that the audience has about what a documentary is – and therefore what it isn't.

So, conventionally, we expect that a documentary will be:
● Non-fiction
● About the real (historical, political, cultural etc events) world
● Unstaged
● Based on observation rather than intervention
● Informative, educational.

It is soon apparent, however, that these definitions only apply to some, often more traditional, documentaries and that the form incorporates a diverse range of styles and aims. Many films routinely defined as documentary do not fit some of the above parameters, for example:

Super Size Me (Morgan Spurlock, US, 2004) is based on a set-up situation – the premise of the documentary (the filmmaker analyses the effect of only eating McDonald's for 30 days) is staged.

Wisconsin Death Trip (James Marsh, US, 1999) is entirely composed of reconstructions of stories taken from a local paper in Wisconsin in the 19th century.

Touching the Void (Kevin MacDonald, UK, 2003) uses reconstructions and expressive film language to recreate the experience of the mountaineers.

At the climax of *Kurt and Courtney* (Nick Broomfield, UK, 1998) the filmmaker directly intervenes in the events, making a speech at a ceremony he was filming.

Worksheets 1 and 2 Defining the documentary – Film and television

These two worksheets – one on film documentaries and one on television forms – help students to build up a resource of examples for reference throughout their study and to start thinking about different categories of documentary. To complete the activities, students need access to television listings magazines, film journals (eg *Sight and Sound* or *Empire*) and/or the internet.

1 of 2 pages

To access student worksheets and other online materials go to *Teaching Film and TV Documentary* at **www.bfi.org.uk/tfms** and enter User name: **docs@bfi.org.uk** and Password: **te1612do**.

Teaching tip

Throughout their study, students should be encouraged to debate definitions and particularly to question how elastic the term documentary is, eg What is the relationship of journalism to documentary? Are home movies a form of documentary? What about news broadcasts? CCTV footage? What is the definition of drama-documentary? What about fiction films and television dramas based on real events?

● Realism

Definitions and debates about realism are central to the study of documentary and can be complex and difficult – as well as a fascinating area for class discussion. For this reason it is useful to introduce some key areas at an early stage which can be referred to and developed throughout the study.

For example, you could use the following questions as the basis for discussion:

- What is meant by the term 'real world'?
- To what extent can film (fiction or non-fiction) reflect the real world?
- If you were a documentary-maker how would you try to capture the real world on film? What techniques would you use?
- What would be some of the obstacles to showing the real world?
- What are some of the differences between the real world as you experience it and the real world as shown on film?

Teaching tip

You could begin to explore the definition of realism as an aesthetic by looking at examples from fiction as well as non-fiction forms. For example the films of realist filmmakers such as Ken Loach, Larry Clark (*Kids*, US, 1996; *The Wassup Rockers*, US, 2005), films which blur the boundaries of fact and fiction, eg *Bullet Boy* (Saul Dibb, UK, 2004), *Kidulthood* (Menaj Huda, UK, 2006), soap operas, as well as extracts from documentaries.

At this stage it is important that students are already thinking about documentary style as a construction, a visual style like any other, rather than a direct representation of reality.

Subjectivity and objectivity

Can a documentary ever be objective? In initial discussions and definitions of documentary it is common for students to conflate the concepts of fact and objectivity, often arguing that documentary has a duty to 'show both sides of the story'. This can actually provide a very useful basis for debate on whether a documentary-maker can ever be completely objective and whether or not they should try to be. Central to this would be the consideration of how subjects are chosen, the use of editing, what is left in and what is left out etc.

Within the historical development of documentary, filmmakers have argued for both the subjective and objective role of the filmmaker. The aim of cinema vérité was for the documentary-maker to become invisible, getting as close as possible to an objective view of the world in reaction against more obviously subjective forms.

Worksheet 3 Defining documentary techniques

To complete the worksheet students need to watch extracts (approximately three minutes each) from a range of documentaries. These examples should come from television and film and take in different styles, institutions, subject matter and audience.

This worksheet provides the basis for the study of documentary techniques that will be built on throughout the guide. Students are asked to describe a range of techniques and to analyse the different functions of these in the context of audience and subject matter.

The skills developed in this worksheet – note-taking and analysis of extracts – are also good preparation for AQA Med 1 and Med 6 and OCR 2731.

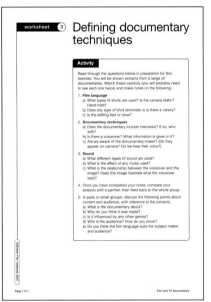

To access student worksheets and other online materials go to *Teaching Film and TV Documentary* at **www.bfi.org.uk/tfms** and enter User name: **docs@bfi.org.uk** and Password: **te1612do**.

Key questions for students

● What is a documentary?
This may seem a straightforward question – we expect a documentary to be a factual film or programme about the real world. However, definitions become more complicated when we consider the development of hybrid forms such as docudrama, docusoap, reality TV etc. How does the mixing of factual and fictional forms affect our definitions? (See Background, Approaches to documentary, p17)

● What techniques do documentaries use? These can include film language, interviews, voiceover, 'found' footage etc

What specific techniques can we identify in documentaries? How do these differ across different kinds of documentary? How does the development of new technology, such as lightweight or hidden cameras, affect the kind of documentaries that can be made? (See Background, Documentary realism and representation, p22)

● Why do you watch documentaries? (If you don't – why not?)

Documentaries are often perceived to be purely educational, often about serious political or cultural events that can seem removed from our own experiences. It is important in defining the purpose of documentary to consider the ways in which documentary forms aim to entertain the audience. This would include the use of explicit techniques in sensational TV documentaries (*The 40 Year Pregnancy*, *The Woman Who Lost 30 Stone* (both Five, 2006)) and strategies such as cliffhangers and enigmas within more 'serious' forms. (See Case study 1)

● Where does the audience watch documentaries?

The range of exhibition and viewing opportunities has obviously changed with the introduction of new technology, from the first cinema screenings of documentary in the silent era to distribution on television, video, DVD and online. The changes in distribution can also indicate the increased popularity of contemporary documentaries and the different target audiences. (See Case study 2)

● What are some of the different aims of documentaries?

Has a documentary affected the way you look at the world or changed your point of view on a particular topic? Do documentary-makers want to persuade the viewer to accept their own point of view? How does this affect the idea that documentaries are a reflection of reality? (See Case study 1)

● Research and resources

The following resources are very useful for research and keeping up to date with recent examples of, and developments in, documentary. Some websites also provide extracts/entire screenings of documentaries (particularly useful for some older examples).

● www.filmguardian.co.uk and www.mediaguardian.co.uk
Printable versions of reviews and features on a range of film and television documentary.

● www.bbc.co.uk/bbcfour/documentaries/storyville/
The *Storyville* homepage provides information about all the documentaries in the *Storyville* strand as well as links to other useful sites (including an interview with Nick Fraser, the series' editor).

- www.channelfour.com/fourdocs/
  Comprehensive resource with documentary timeline, extensive archive of complete films and extracts to watch, interviews with documentary-makers, reviews etc. Also gives students the opportunity to upload their own documentaries to be screened on the website.

- www.screenonline.org.uk
  The BFI's educational resource with detailed information on documentary movements, periods and individual filmmakers for British film and television. Extracts from a variety of documentaries are also available online.

How to use this guide

This guide is structured to integrate theoretical approaches with specific examples (in some cases this might include practical production work) and to encourage students to consider a range of Film and Media Studies debates within the context of the study of documentary. The activities and suggestions for further work are designed to help students to construct their own analysis and develop ideas within the demands of the Film and Media Studies specifications.

The Background provides an historical and theoretical context for the study of documentary through the Timeline and a discussion of the important theoretical debates, including those around realism and representation. The significant developments in theoretical approaches are summarised in an accessible way and there are teaching tips and suggestions for further work to help students' understanding.

The three case studies in the final section are structured thematically, pulling together a wide range of examples to create new ways of looking at documentary; making connections across different periods and styles. The case studies are:

Case study 1: Documentary, propaganda and social and political change
This case study uses historical and contemporary examples to examine the way in which documentary has been used to try to change the audience's views and behaviour. Examples include the British documentary film movement of the 1930s and contemporary campaigning documentaries such as *Super Size Me* (Morgan Spurlock, US, 2004) and *Jamie's School Dinners* (Channel 4, 2005).

Case study 2: Observational documentary and the new television formats
Beginning with the American direct cinema movement of the 1960s, this case study traces the way in which the techniques developed in that period have been used for very different types of television formats such as docusoaps and reality television (*Big Brother*, Channel 4, 2000–present).

Case study 3: Documentary and performance

Traditional definitions of documentary rely on the idea that documentary is 'unstaged'; here the link between documentary and performance is examined in the films of Nick Broomfield (*Kurt and Courtney*, UK, 1998*; Aileen: Life and Death of a Serial Killer*, UK, 2004) – where the documentary-maker becomes the star of his own films. Another concept of performance is apparent in the category of drama-documentary, which uses techniques more usually associated with fiction forms, examined in reference to the recent work of Paul Greengrass (*Bloody Sunday*, UK, 2002; *United 93*, US/UK/France, 2006).

The activities in the worksheets develop students' skills through analysis of film language and documentary techniques as well as the wider institutional and economic contexts. These activities are available as online worksheets. To access the worksheets and other online materials go to *Teaching Film and TV Documentary* at www.bfi.org.uk/tfms and enter: Username: **docs@bfi.org.uk** Password: **te1612do**

The following schemes of work illustrate the way you could 'pick and mix' from the guide.

Scheme of work 1: Documentary realism and representation

Central to this scheme of work is the definition of realism and representation in documentary – specifically the concept of documentary realism as a construction. The discussion of realism and representation is aimed at AS Level students through introductory textual analysis exercises, but can be developed for A2 students.

Aims:
To promote understanding and awareness of:
- A range of documentary techniques
- The conventions of documentary realism
- The representation of groups, people, places etc.

Outcomes:
- To produce a comparative analysis of realist techniques
- To develop an analysis of representation in documentary.

● Week 1 Defining documentary

Definitions and debates around what a documentary is, with reference to subject matter, film language, the role of the documentary-maker
(Worksheets 1 and **2)**

- ## Week 2 Documentary realism and film language

Definitions of realism in film, formalists and realists, the indexical bond.
Analysis of techniques, including film language, present and distant effects
(Worksheets 3 and 4)

- ## Week 3 Documentary modes

Definitions of different modes, role of the documentary-maker, examination of
subject matter
(Worksheets 5 and 6)

- ## Week 4 Case study: Observational documentary

Conventions and context of observational documentary
Close textual study: *Être et Avoir*
(Worksheets 11, 12 and 13)

- ## Week 5 Popular factual programming (1)

Conventions and context of the docusoaps
Comparative analysis with observational modes, hybrid genres and use of
fictional techniques
Student research into current docusoaps, representation of people and places
Worksheets 14 and 15

- ## Week 6 Popular factual programming (2)

Conventions and context of reality television
Comparative analysis with other modes of factual television (genre and
representation)
Institutional contexts and convergence
(Worksheets 16 and 17)

Scheme of work 2:
Documentary, propaganda and persuasion

This scheme of work develops the study of documentary through an analysis
of the ways in which the form has been used for propaganda, persuasion and
campaigning purposes. This includes a range of government/state and
individual examples, the filmic conventions associated with the form and
debates the meaning and distinctions of the different terms. It is aimed at A2
students who will be familiar with documentary techniques as well as the
concepts of ideology and audience that underpin this scheme.

Aims:

To promote understanding and awareness of:

- Definitions of propaganda
- Persuasive techniques
- The relationship between producers, audience and text.

Outcomes:

- To produce a comparative analysis of different types of propaganda, persuasion, campaigning documentary
- To provide a critical reading of the ideological function of documentary techniques.

● Week 1 Defining propaganda and persuasion

Historical context, state and corporate propaganda
Case study of *Outfoxed* (Robert Greenwald, US, 2004)

● Week 2 British documentary movement

Historical and social context, Grierson and definitions of documentary, concept of 'good propaganda'
Focus film: *Night Mail* (Harry Watt and Basil Wright, UK, 1936), analysis of representations for propaganda purposes
(Worksheets 6 and **7)**

● Week 3 Documentary and social protest

Distinction between protest, campaigning and propaganda (De Nitto's categories)
Analysis of a range of campaigning documentaries and the reason for their increased popularity (single-issue politics etc)

● Week 4 Focus film: *Super Size Me* (and *Jamie's School Dinners*)

Close study of persuasive techniques; link between film language and presenting an argument, mode of address
Definition of different examples of subjectivity in documentary
(Worksheets: 9 and **10)**

● Week 5 Subjectivity and performative documentary

Close study: Nick Broomfield
Defining the performative mode, debating the role of the filmmaker, audience manipulation.
(Worksheets 19 and **20)**

● Week 6 Campaigning and investigative forms

Close study of the drama-documentary, genre and filmic conventions
Social and political aims; the work of Paul Greengrass
(Worksheet 21)

2

Background

Timeline

To provide an historical perspective, a timeline outlining the history of the documentary form is available at www.bfi.org.uk/tfms. Go to the page for *Teaching Film and TV Documentary*, and enter username: docs@bfi.org.uk, Password: te1612do

Approaches to documentary

Discussion and analysis of documentary forms usually draw on a range of approaches that can be identified as follows:

- Realism and documentary
- Audience interpretation
- Modes of documentary
- Documentary versus fiction
- Function of documentary
- Documentary and ethics.

● Realism and documentary

Central to this aspect of the study of documentary is the way that it records but also transforms reality through a range of film language and construction techniques: the documentary discourse.

Documentary has a specific relationship with the real world. There is an assumption that a documentary will engage with events in the real world – the political, social, historical sphere – rather than be the product of the imagination. The question of how documentary can best represent reality has been central to the making and study of documentary from the beginning; John Grierson was not interested in 'shapeless reproduction', seeing himself rather as an artist creating a work of art.

The current trend for hybrid forms introducing fictional techniques is actually nothing new. The history of documentary is full of examples of reconstruction and invention, eg *Nanook of the North* (Robert Flaherty, US/France, 1922). This fluid mixing of fact and fiction makes the documentary form more interesting, with documentaries sometimes using actors, special effects, emotional music and reconstructions, eg *Touching the Void* (Kevin MacDonald, UK, 2003), while fiction films use non-actors, long takes and little dialogue, eg *Bubble* (Steven Soderbergh, US, 2006).

● Audience interpretation

How does the audience interpret documentary? The documentary form is based on a very close relationship between reality and the image. The term document originally carried with it the connotation of evidence, a meaning which has passed from legal documents, to the photograph and then to film. It is this concept of evidence which gives the documentary its ideological power. What happens when these assumptions are questioned? How has the development of new technology and the ability to manipulate the image affected the audience's belief in the truth of documentary?

This increased scepticism towards the documentary can be seen partly as a result of 'mock' documentaries. In television, these include *The Office* (BBC, 2001–3), a sitcom in the form of a docusoap and *Curb Your Enthusiasm* (HBO, 2000–present) a sitcom where the actors 'play themselves', with scenes improvised and filmed in documentary style. In cinema, films such as *The Blair Witch Project* (Daniel Myrick and Eduardo Sanchez, US, 1999) and *The Last Broadcast* (Stefan Avalos and Lance Weiler, US, 1998) used documentary techniques – and were promoted as being real – to tell a fictional story. The recent release of *Unknown White Male* (Rupert Murray, US, 2006) is further evidence of this distrust between the audience and the documentary producer. *Unknown White Male* documents the experiences of a man with retrograde amnesia – he cannot remember anything that happened to him before July 2003. The rarity of this condition has led some – critics, doctors and other filmmakers – to question the authenticity of his illness and therefore the documentary itself. The resulting controversy has become part of the discussion of the film and thus affects the audience interpretation. The changing relationship between the documentary and the audience can also be seen as indicative of the wider context of postmodernism, where the idea of objective truth and the validity of the image is continually questioned.

● Modes of documentary

An influential approach to the study of documentary has been Nichols' (1991) identification of five different modes – or types – of documentary. This is a way of organising documentary into categories – there are similarities with the use of genre categories in fiction film. However, unlike genre categories, modes are defined with reference to documentary techniques rather than subject matter etc. The five modes will be discussed in greater detail but can be categorised in the following way:

1. Expository documentary
This type of documentary is probably the most familiar to audiences and tends to be more commonly seen on TV rather than in documentaries made for the cinema. The documentary techniques used include a voiceover narration, commenting on the images and explaining what is happening in a direct address to the audience. The aim of an expository documentary is usually to inform the audience about a place, an event etc with which they are not familiar. Usually an expository documentary will develop an argument – it is not objective.

2. Observational documentary
This type of documentary can also be referred to as 'fly-on-the-wall' and it attempts to represent the world as it is. Techniques include long takes, hand-held camera, with no interviews or voiceover, in an attempt to capture a slice of life. In the observational documentary, the audience should not be aware of the filmmaker, making it very different from other modes such as the participatory documentary.

3. Participatory (interactive) documentary
In opposition to the observational style, the filmmaker is foregrounded in the participatory mode, making it explicit that the film is made from their point of view. The filmmaker is often the central character in the film with the emphasis on their interaction with the people that they meet and these people's reaction to them. Techniques include filmmaker's voiceover (with pronounced use of 'I'), hand-held camera and an emphasis on informal interviews.

4. Reflexive documentary

5. Performative documentary

The final two modes are linked because they both investigate the relationship between the real world and the way in which documentaries represent it. Reflexive documentary reveals how documentaries are produced as representations based on the construction and manipulation of the image. The performative documentary takes this idea further, explicitly challenging the idea of documentary truth, emphasising instead the process of film language itself.

These categories, particularly the last two, are interpreted differently by different critics and should be seen as a basis for debate and argument. Again the analogy with genre categories is useful here; there isn't always a consensus about which film fits which genre. It is also worth noting that recent developments in documentary styles will affect the relevance of the categories.

● Documentary versus fiction

Despite the particular relationship to reality, documentary uses many techniques from fiction filmmaking. All documentaries employ some form of structuring device to help shape the information for the audience and these devices are close to the narrative structures found in fiction. These techniques include setting up a 'problem' at the beginning of the film (How did Kurt Cobain die? Who will win the spelling bee?) which is – usually – followed through to a resolution. The selection of material by the documentary-maker is done to encourage the audience to identify with particular 'characters' in the film, sometimes in opposition to others.

Audience expectations in relation to fiction and non-fiction forms have also changed. In 1914 the photographer Edward Sherriff Curtis decided to make a film documentary about the 'Indian and Indian life' which he had photographed in North America. In his proposal for funding he stated:

> The question might be raised as to whether the documentary material would not lack the thrilling interest of the fake [fiction] picture ... (Holm and Quimby, 1980)

This concern seems to be very different from the contemporary experience, with one of the attractions for the audience being the emphasis – particularly in TV formats – on the reality of what is being depicted.

The distinction between fiction and non-fiction film also raises questions about the cultural and artistic status of the forms, with documentary often being perceived (not least by documentary-makers themselves) as a more serious and more enduring form compared to fiction films which offer more immediate but transitory pleasures.

● Function of documentary

Documentary can fulfil a variety of functions which are partly dependent on the institutional context of the film or programme. There has always been an expectation that the documentary will have an educational function, ie enlighten the audience in some way. This concept of the social function of documentary has been evident since the 1920s with Grierson's belief that documentary could perform a democratic function – educating the ordinary citizen about wider social, political and cultural developments. Many documentary-makers have seen their role as a campaigning one: investigating social inequalities and miscarriages of justice. The success of this aim of documentary is difficult to judge as examples of a documentary leading directly to social or political change are rare. However, it is possible to make the case for *The Thin Blue Line* (Errol Morris, US, 1989), which led to a man being released from death row, as well as *Jamie's School Dinners* which led to a government review of the nutritional value of school meals. The recent work of Mark Daly, *The Secret Policeman* (BBC, 2003) and *The Boys Who Killed Stephen Lawrence* (BBC, 2006), have both led to police enquiries.

● Documentary and ethics

The making – and watching – of documentaries does raise the question of ethics. Is the documentary intrusive? Voyeuristic? What happened to the subject once the documentary-maker left? How can the documentary-maker avoid taking advantage of the subject? What is the balance between the audience's right to know and the participant's right to privacy?

There is a legal framework which does offer guidance in addressing some of these questions. There are two relevant legal positions (in general terms):

1. The relationship of the filmmaker to the participants – concept of consent.

2   The relationship of the filmmaker to the film – copyright.

Consent by a participant to be filmed for a documentary must be voluntary and informed. Informed consent implies that a participant must understand the potential damage which could be caused – including psychological damage through distress. The definition of informed consent becomes more difficult in the case of children – the documentary is likely still to be seen once they are adults – or those who are not mentally capable of giving consent at the time of filming. This was the case with Frederick Wiseman's *Titticut Follies* (US, 1967), an observational documentary about the patients in a mental institution.

The question of copyright also raises interesting ethical issues: Who owns the image? The participant or the filmmaker? This question has been central to the legal dispute over *Être et Avoir* (Nicholas Philibert, France, 2002). This film explores the life of a rural French school through the relationships between the local families, the students and the teacher, Georges Lopez. After the commercial success of the film, Lopez sued the filmmakers for a share of the profits, arguing that he was an 'actor' in the film. The legal ruling (April 2006) found in favour of the filmmaker, stating that the subject matter was the property of the director alone, therefore granting him the copyright to the images of the teacher. (See Case study 2 for more on *Être et avoir*)

Documentary realism and representation

In the next section, we cover in more detail documentary realism and representation.

- How is documentary realism different from and similar to other forms of realism?
- Can documentary directly reflect reality?
- What is the role of the filmmaker?
- What realist techniques do documentaries use? How have these changed over time?
- The link between realism and ideology
- The function of documentary realism.

● Realism and cinema

The ability of film – a form of mechanical reproduction – to capture the real world was one of the first attractions of the new medium for audiences at the end of the 19th century. The first audiences for film, or the cinematograph, went to see a version of their own recognisable world on screen, rather than a fantasy. Louis Lumière's (the French filmmaker and inventor of the cinematograph) first films, *Arrival of a Train* (France, 1895) and *Workers Leaving the Factory* (France, 1895) were popular with audiences because they were a direct recording of reality, an everyday event, but one which was transformed through the use of unfamiliar cinematic techniques; for example, the depth of field and movement, which distinguished it from previous experiences of the theatre or of stills photography. Lumière's films, often less than a minute long, were arguably the first documentaries – recordings of unstaged events in the real world – and combined the sense of the familiar (the real world) and the strange (the use of cinematic techniques), a combination that has remained central to the appeal of the documentary.

● Realism and film language

The dominant film language style as it developed in the first part of the 20th century is a realist one; films, whether fiction or non-fiction, are recognisable representations of the world.

However, film is capable of both

- Perfectly recording reality
- Transforming reality in an expressive way.

In the history of cinema, filmmakers and theorists have debated whether film should be used for the first or second function. These positions were defined as realist (film was unique because it had a direct connection with the real world) and formalist (film language should be used to construct the filmmaker's view of the world). Each position had specific film-language techniques associated with it:

- Realism: the long take, deep-focus photography, static, eye-level camera shots
- Formalism: editing, montage, slowing down and speeding up film stock, high and low camera angles.

Discussion points

Students should consider:

- Which techniques come closer to representing reality?
- How would the use of new technology such as lightweight, hand-held cameras affect the above techniques?
- Is there a difference in the function of the director in the two styles?

Teaching tip

To illustrate this argument it is helpful to show some examples of different types of film styles, eg

- Realism
  Citizen Kane (Orson Welles, US, 1941), *The Magnificent Ambersons* (Orson Welles, US, 1942), *Bubble* (Steven Soderbergh, US, 2006), *Festen* (Thomas Vinterberg, Denmark, 1997), *Elephant* (Gus Van Sant, US, 2004).

- Formalism
  Psycho (particularly the shower sequence, Alfred Hitchcock, US, 1960), *Battleship Potemkin* (Sergei Eisenstein, USSR, 1925), *Man with the Movie Camera* (Dziga Vertov, USSR, 1929), *The Thin Blue Line* (Errol Morris, US, 1989).

The two different styles develop from different conceptions of the role of the filmmaker: the first features minimal intervention by the director; in the second the director is wholly responsible for the construction of the finished film from the raw material shot. The relationship of the filmmaker to the material is central in discussing the role of the documentary-maker and whether or not documentaries can ever be objective.

André Bazin argued that film was an art form precisely because it could capture the way in which we see the world, that it fulfilled the audience's

> appetite for illusion by a mechanical reproduction in the making of which man plays no part. (Bazin, 1960)

● Andy Warhol and *Empire*

The pop artist and avant-garde filmmaker, Andy Warhol, explored the relationship between the artist and the work of art throughout his career and across different artistic media. In his work as a filmmaker he subverted the concept of the director as *auteur*, rejecting the idea of the filmmaker as artist. Instead he attempted to record the world without intervention from the filmmaker, a process that has been referred to as 'the dehumanization of the cinematic eye' (Koch, 1991). The most famous example of this is the film *Empire* (US, 1964), an eight-hour, black-and-white, static shot film of the Empire State Building, filmed from one position, the 44th floor of the Time-Life building. The film has no conventional content or plot but instead records the changing light on the Empire State Building over the hours from dusk until morning. Often described as a film to be thought about rather than seen (a definition of conceptual art), *Empire* does raise interesting questions about the definition of documentary and the idea of objectivity.

You can watch an extract of *Empire* at:
www.medienkunstnetz.de/works/empire/video/1/#reiter

Discussion points

- Is Warhol successful in this 'dehumanization of the cinematic eye'? What evidence of the director would there be in the finished film (consider the choice of subject matter)?
- How realistic is *Empire*?
- Does *Empire* reflect the way we look at the world?
- Can *Empire* be defined as a documentary?
- What do you think it would be like to watch it?

The concept of 'man playing no part' is relevant to the belief that what film shows is the original object itself – unaltered by the filmmaker's perspective or intervention. This definition of film realism suggests that there is almost no mediation involved in the filming of the real world.

● The indexical bond

The link between the photographic image – still or moving – and the real world is analysed in semiology, the study of signs. This is a very complex area which students at this level do not need to go into in great detail; however, some of the concepts are relevant and should make for an interesting discussion about the relationship between images and the objects they represent.

Charles Pierce defined the photographic image as an example of an indexical bond; it has a physical connection to the object it reproduces. It is this that gives photography its status as evidence – it appears authentic.

Christian Metz developed these ideas in relation to cinema, arguing that

> A close-up of a revolver does not signify 'revolver' … but signifies as a
> minimum, leaving aside its connotations, 'Here is a revolver.' It carries
> with it its own actualisation, a kind of 'Here is'. (Metz in Wollen, 1972)

Both these views emphasise the immediacy of the photographic image and its
direct relationship to the object being filmed:

> there is no human intervention, no transformation, no code, between the
> object and the sign; hence the paradox that the photograph is a
> message without a code. (Wollen, 1972)

However, this idea of authenticity is questionable because:

- The photographic image captures an object, place etc only at a specific
  time and may not be representative of it
- The indexical bond relationship also applies to fiction film; a studio set may
  be created to convince as a 19th-century street etc.

The capacity for recording the real world in an immediate way is central to the
aesthetic of documentary realism.

● Documentary realism: present and distant

The function of documentary realism is to create the illusion of the immediacy
of events for the viewer, to hide the contradiction inherent in the form:

> Realism is a construction, therefore it is impossible to achieve a perfect
> match between events in the real world and the text that represents
> them. (Izod and Kilborn, 1997, p42)

In order to create the illusion of reality, the documentary discourse (the use of
particular conventions) places the audience in a seemingly contradictory
position, creating the feeling of being simultaneously present at and distant
from the action, taking up the position of both participant and observer.
Therefore the documentary lets the audience feel part of the action ('as if I was
there'), but also to react as an expert, retaining the critical distance necessary
to judge the events taking place. In this way the audience experience seems
to mirror that of the documentary-maker, who is present at the events,
documenting things as they happen but also distant from them, commenting
and shaping them to present them to an audience – the role of the expert.

● Conventions of documentary realism

Documentary-makers may have different individual styles but most can be
classed as realist – they aim to convince the audience of the truthfulness of
what they have recorded. Because of this, documentary realism tends to be
characterised by minimal use of experimental or expressive techniques,

instead employing conventions which aim to convince the audience that what they are watching is authentic. (There are exceptions to this style eg *Man with the Movie Camera* and *The Thin Blue Line*, but these can be seen as 'exceptions which prove the rule'.)

> Documentary realism is the style that has characterised documentary more than any other. (Nichols in Izod et al, 2000, p91)

This is a useful quotation as it emphasises the fact that documentary realism is a style constructed of particular conventions, rather than a natural or inevitable result of documentary-making. As with any form of realism, the conventions of documentary realism are not fixed and will change over time; they are historically specific and develop in relation to changing values and attitudes in society.

Film language

There are certain conventions of film language that can be identified as part of documentary realism. These conventions are part of the way in which the audience experience of feeling both present and distant from events is constructed.

Present: techniques of film language which enhance the audience's sense of 'being there' (not all the techniques will be present in all documentaries):

- Location shooting
- Uneven, hand-held camerawork
- Natural lighting
- Following the action
- Filmmaker's visible presence
- Synchronous sound recording
- Interviews with witnesses
- Editing placing audience 'in' the scene
- Overall visual effect of an amateur rather than a professional production.

Overall, these conventions aim to create a sense of immediacy with events unfolding in real time.

Distant: techniques that allow the audience to feel objective about the subject:

- Voiceover narration
- Use of archive material (stills, news footage) and research
- Expert testimony
- Material shaped into a narrative
- Material structured into an argument.

Overall, these conventions aim to make the audience feel in control of the material and that they have expert knowledge.

The concept of feeling both present and distant could also be defined in the following way:

- Present: intimate, often emotional reaction, close engagement with the subject
- Distant: removed from the subject, with this detachment seen as necessary for the viewer to remain objective and able to make a judgement about the information presented.

Summary

- These filmic conventions of documentary realism create an emotional engagement for the audience but also allow for a more dispassionate response.
- The need for distance is also true for the filmmaker whose judgement may be questioned if they become too close to the subject matter.
- One of the reasons for the need for objectivity – or appearance of it – in documentary may be to do with the demands of the institutional context eg broadcasters must comply with broadcasting legislation.

Worksheet 4 Techniques of documentary realism: Distant and present effects

Film extract: *Spellbound* (Jeffrey Blitz, US, 2003). From the intertitle, 'Perryton, Texas' (approximately two minutes from the beginning, to the end of this section, eight minutes in total).

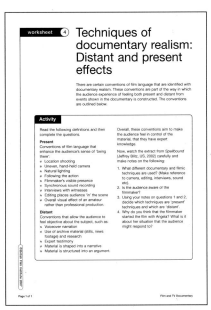

To access student worksheets and other online materials go to *Teaching Film and TV Documentary* at **www.bfi.org.uk/tfms** and enter User name: **docs@bfi.org.uk** and Password: **te1612do**.

This worksheet uses an extract from the documentary *Spellbound* to analyse the way that the filmmaker uses present and distant techniques to represent the experiences of young students who have entered the US national spelling bee. (The popularity of the film was evident when the BBC launched a Saturday night interactive spelling competition in the wake of its release.) The worksheet could form part of a wider study of this documentary or could be adapted to be used with other examples.

Points to note in the extract

- A range of techniques is evident: interviews, location shooting, hand-held camera, use of archive and news footage.
- Some can be defined as 'present' techniques (location shooting, presence of the filmmaker in interviews, interviews with people involved).
- Techniques with a more distancing effect include the use of intertitles, non-diegetic music, news footage, manipulation of the film stock (fast-cutting and sound distortion). It could be argued that the translation of the father's words (rather than showing him speaking directly to camera) is also distancing.
- The film of the regional spelling competition starts in fly-on-the-wall style but, as the competition reaches the final stages, the editing speeds up to create tension (a technique repeated at the national competition).
- The intertitles are used throughout the film, as a structuring device to introduce the characters. Each section follows the same pattern: the student at school, with friends, with family and training for the competition.

● Documentary realism and ideology

In analysing the conventions of documentary realism it is also important to question why this particular style developed and how the audience interprets it. The audience of a documentary is already expecting the conventions of realism before the film or programme starts and is therefore primed to accept the images as real, as authentic. The appeal of the documentary form also relies on the promise that the viewer will discover something, learn something in the process, an appeal that aids the work of the documentary-maker – the audience wants to believe what it sees. This context of style and audience expectation means that documentaries can be a powerful ideological tool – their ideological message is rendered invisible because they are accepted as just showing the world 'as it is'. This relies on the acceptance by the audience that the documentary images are a direct reflection of reality and not a mediated construction.

Teaching tip

It is often easier to analyse documentaries as ideological constructions by studying documentaries from previous eras that do not elicit the same recognition of the real world in contemporary audiences. The films of the British documentary movement of the 1930s – such as *Night Mail* (Harry Watt and Basil Wright, UK, 1936) – may have seemed realistic to a contemporary audience (although even this is an assumption which could be debated) but now we are likely to recognise the representations of class and gender as ideological constructs – as well as patronising and out of step with our own values.

The ideological power of the documentary – and its use as propaganda – relies in part on the audience's faith in its authenticity. It is debatable whether that is still the case with the contemporary audience's knowledge of the potential of new technology for 'faking' and reconstructions etc. It may well be the case that documentaries are now consumed with more scepticism than acceptance of the relationship between the image and the real world.

Modes of documentary

This section examines the different documentary modes in detail.

Identifying the different modes of documentary representation has become one of the dominant approaches in this area of study. There are many useful aspects to this approach but dividing documentaries into modes can also be a restricting – and at times confusing – activity.

Teaching tip

In using the modes in teaching it is useful to get students to identify the techniques and conventions in a range of documentaries **(Worksheets 3** and **4)** first and then to think about which mode is dominant – rather than trying to fit the modes to the examples.

It is also important to be aware of some issues that will arise in this process:

- It can be difficult to distinguish between different modes – there are areas of overlap.
- It is better to approach the categorisation of a documentary through identifying which mode is dominant rather than expecting to find all the techniques present.
- Some documentaries can be placed in more than one mode.
- The category of documentary as a whole is fluid and can be difficult to define.
- The terms used for some of the modes, particularly reflexive, interactive and performative can have different meanings in different contexts.
- Theorists don't always agree as to which mode a documentary belongs.

It is important to be able to identify the different modes in documentary but also to be aware of why these types of category have been developed and what they tell us about the relationship between documentary and reality.

● Bill Nichols: Representing reality and blurred boundaries

Bill Nichols is one of the key theorists in the study of documentary. He identified the modes of representation – defined as 'basic ways of organising texts in relation to certain recurrent features or conventions' – that have since been debated, argued over and added to. In *Representing Reality* (1991), Nichols identified four dominant organisational patterns in documentary: expository, observational, interactive and reflexive. In *Blurred Boundaries* (1994), this was expanded to include poetic as an early form (1920s) and performative as a recent development in documentary style. In Nichols' *Introduction to Documentary* (2001), the interactive mode is renamed as participatory – perhaps to avoid confusion with the reflexive mode and also in recognition of a change in the use of the term interactive in the wider culture.

Nichols' work is sometimes attacked (see Bruzzi, 2000) for being rigid and prescriptive. He does, however, emphasise that the modes tend to be combined and altered in individual films and that older categories do not disappear with the introduction of new modes.

● Development of modes

Why do new modes of representation within documentary emerge? Nichols identifies the modes as developing chronologically – although he emphasises that they only provide a partial history of documentary – and in reaction to the limitations of the previous mode.

In studying the development of new modes, it is apparent that a range of contextual factors affects this development – new technology, institutions and audience. This section concentrates on five of the modes as being the most relevant to study. Rather than initially defining them through techniques and conventions, it is helpful to introduce the concept of different modes of representation in terms of understanding the role of the documentary-maker.

In this approach the five modes can be divided into two groups:

● **Group A:** Expository, observational
● **Group B:** Participatory, reflexive, performative.

In Group A, the documentaries claim to be revealing the world as it is (although they use different techniques to achieve this) and make direct reference to the real world. In both the modes in this group the organising work and mediation of the filmmaker is hidden. In expository documentary this is done through the authoritative 'voice of God' narration, in observational through the capturing of events as they happen. In Group B, the documentary-maker's presence becomes evident, the process of filmmaking itself becomes the subject as much as – in some cases more than – the references to the real world.

Summary

- Group A attempts to hide the role of the filmmaker and emphasises the filmmaker's interpretation of the world.
- Group B foregrounds the role of the filmmaker and shifts the emphasis to the way that the audience interprets the film.

One way to use the modes of representation is to discuss the way in which they develop out of the documentary-maker's own need to signal their participation in the filmmaking process. This has many implications for the idea of documentary as objective or truthful, which is illustrated by Nichols' discussion of *Nanook of the North*. The audience is told that Nanook and his family will starve if he is unable to find food but the audience doesn't know what Flaherty and his family ate or if he offered food to Nanook. Nichols argues that this is a kind of dishonesty on the part of the filmmaker and compares it to later modes of documentary:

> With filmmakers like Jean Rouch (*Chronicle of a Summer*, Jean Rouch and Edgar Morin, France, 1961), Nick Broomfield (*Aileen Wournos: The Selling of a Serial Killer*, UK, 1992) … what happens because of the filmmaker's presence becomes as crucial as anything that happens despite his presence. (2001)

Students could analyse the role of the documentary-maker by asking the following questions:

- Is the audience aware of the documentary-maker?
- Do they interview subjects?
- Do they provide the voiceover?
- Do we know what their reaction to the subject matter is?
- Do they explain the different stages and processes of the filmmaking?

The following section outlines the main documentary modes and suggests reasons for their development. All the dominant conventions are in place by the participatory mode – reflexive and performative documentary use a mixture of techniques found in the previous modes.

● Expository conventions

- Voiceover addresses the audience directly and is the dominant convention.
- The voiceover may either be a 'voice of God' commentator (heard but not seen) or 'voice of authority' (seen and heard – usually an expert in the relevant field).

- Images are used to illustrate (or sometimes counterpoint) the voiceover.
- Direct relationship between voiceover and images shown.
- Editing is used for continuity, to link together images supporting the argument put forward in the voiceover.
- A variety of footage, interviews, stills and archive material are assembled to support the argument.
- There is an attempt to persuade the audience of a particular point of view, often by appealing to logic and the idea of a common-sense response.
- Events are organised to provide the viewer with the solution to a puzzle.

Contextual factors

In the 1920s the technology for recording sound on location (synchronous sound) was limited which may be one reason for the use of a voiceover, which could be recorded in the studio. However, the expository mode can also be interpreted as representative of wider social and cultural contexts of the time; the authoritative and instructional tone of early documentary has been linked to a hierarchical society where the dominant groups felt it their responsibility to teach the masses. It also suggests a greater trust in authority and experts than is evident now.

Teaching tip

Several areas of debate arise from this analysis:

- Can a style (this could be widened to consider all areas of the media) be explained solely through reference to new technology?
- If expository documentary is the product of a particular time and place, why is it so popular (particularly on TV) today?
- The concept of early documentary as an educational tool is also seen in the contemporaneous development of the Reithian ideology of public service broadcasting.

● Observational conventions

- Location shooting; hand-held cameras.
- Long takes dominate.
- Synchronous sound recording.
- No voiceover (in its purest form).
- No interviews.
- Documentary-maker's presence is hidden.
- Subjects pretend that they are not being filmed.

Contextual factors

The development of the observational mode is often linked to the development of new technology, specifically the hand-held camera and audiotape machines which facilitated recording on location, although of dubious quality. This mode of documentary also developed out of a political culture – a more liberal and open society represented by the mass movements for civil rights of the period. Many observational filmmakers were motivated by the desire for political change but rather than attempting to instruct the audience – as with the expository mode – the observational mode was chosen as being more democratic, allowing audiences to interpret the evidence rather than telling them what to think. Kilborn and Izod (1997) also point to the influence of the new US television networks that developed observational formats in the belief that they would be a ratings winner – they weren't.

● Participatory (interactive) conventions

- Documentary-maker and crew interact with the subject.
- Interviews dominate but tend to be informal – literally 'on the run' questioning.
- Use of archive material – stills, news footage, newspaper headlines, letters etc.
- Location shooting; hand-held camera.
- Long takes dominate.
- Synchronous sound recording.
- Voiceover, usually by the documentary-maker.
- Documentary-maker is visible to the audience – intervenes and participates in the action.

Contextual factors

From the list of conventions, it is clear that there are overlaps between participatory and observational modes; both were made possible by developments in new technology. The participatory mode can be seen as a direct response to the convention (similar to that of fiction film) of hiding the role of the filmmaker in order to help the audience suspend its disbelief – to forget it is watching a film. By revealing the presence of the filmmaker, the participatory mode raises new questions: How far should the intervention go? How much has the participation of the filmmaker altered the behaviour of the subjects? What effect does the participation have on the filmmaker? Does it affect what they decide to leave in and take out of the finished film?

● Reflexive conventions

- Borrows techniques from fiction film for an emotional, subjective response.
- Emphasises the expressive nature of film; anti-realist techniques eg re-enactments, expressive lighting, dramatic music etc.

- Voiceover (when present) is likely to be questioning and uncertain – rather than authoritative.
- Reliance on suggestion rather than fact.
- More iconic than indexical – a move away from documentary's reference to the real world.

Contextual factors

The term reflexive is used to describe this mode due to the foregrounding of film language to represent the subject matter (rather than realism). It is useful to place reflexive documentary in the wider context of postmodern style. The reflexive mode is characterised by the questioning of traditional definitions of knowledge and understanding and the suggestion that emotion, feeling and atmosphere – as well as facts – informs our view of the world. In the context of more traditional expectations of documentary, this is what makes the reflexive mode controversial.

Also controversial is its explicit appeal to audience emotion and subjectivity, which raises concerns about its move away from referencing the real world – the traditional role of documentary.

> Most documentary production concerns itself with talking about the historical world, the reflexive mode addresses the question of how we talk about the historical world. (Nichols, 1991)

● Performative conventions

- Documentary-maker and crew interact with the subject.
- Documentary-maker comments on the process of making the documentary.
- The documentary is often shaped into the narrative of an investigation or search, possibly without a satisfactory conclusion.
- The audience is addressed in an emotional and direct way.
- Subject matter often concerns identity (gender, sexuality) rather than 'factual' topics.

Contextual factors

The performative mode develops the questions raised about the function of the documentary-maker in the participatory form, foregrounding the way in which documentary represents the real world. While the participatory documentary analyses the process through the interaction between subject and filmmaker, in the performative documentary the emphasis is shifted to force the audience to analyse *how* the interaction is represented. Although it emerged in the 1980s, this mode has a lot in common with the politically motivated art movements of the 1960s. These were influenced by Brecht's theory of alienation, which involved revealing the work as a construction and denying the suspension of disbelief. This mode can also be defined as postmodern in its emphasis on gender issues and in giving a voice to groups who had previously been marginalised or spoken for:

> Performative documentary can act as a corrective to those films where 'We speak about them to us'. They proclaim instead that 'We speak about ourselves to you' or 'We speak about ourselves to us'. (Nichols, 1991)

Worksheets 5 and 6: Defining the modes of documentary

These worksheets ask students to analyse documentaries in the context of the different modes and to discuss why a particular mode has been used for a particular content. These worksheets could be used with the extracts that students analysed in Worksheets 1 and 2. **Worksheet 6** asks students to write a proposal for a specific documentary mode.

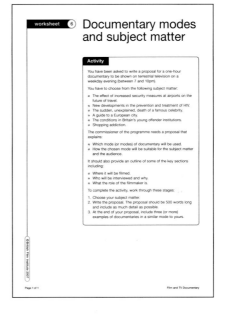

1 of 2 pages

To access student worksheets and other online materials go to *Teaching Film and TV Documentary* at **www.bfi.org.uk/tfms** and enter User name: **docs@bfi.org.uk** and Password: **te1612do**.

3

Case studies

These case studies are organised around themes as follows:

- *Case study 1: Documentary, propaganda and social and political change*
  This case study explores the way that documentary has been used for propaganda, persuasion and campaigning purposes through historical (British documentary film of the 1930s) and contemporary (*Super Size Me*) examples.

- *Case study 2: Observational documentary and the new television formats*
  Beginning with the American Direct cinema movement of the 1960s, this case study analyses the stylistic links between observational documentary techniques and contemporary television formats such as the docusoaps and reality television.

- *Case study 3: Documentary and performance*
  While the study of documentary is often dominated by its relationship to the real world, this case study discusses the way that documentaries can also be constructions that use the same techniques as fiction films. Examples include the work of Nick Broomfield and the drama-documentary.

Case study 1: Documentary, propaganda and social and political change

The role of documentary as a force for social and political change is one which has been associated with the form since the 1930s. Examples include state propaganda and personal polemic and can be found across the different modes of documentary (although historically propaganda was linked to the expository style and currently the participatory documentary is used for campaigning on social and political issues, eg *Fahrenheit 9/11*, Michael Moore, US, 2004; *An Inconvenient Truth*, Davis Guggenheim, US, 2006). This area is still a controversial one and therefore raises many areas for debate – not least in the different definitions of propaganda.

Questions to consider:

- Can a documentary persuade someone to think differently about an event, a place, a person, a political perspective etc?
- What is the context in which the documentary is being interpreted? What other information is there about the subject in society? Who is behind the documentary? Who is the audience?
- What will be the effect on audiences if they are persuaded by the documentary's argument? Will they change their behaviour?
- What is the difference between a documentary produced by the state (the government) or by an individual when the intention is to persuade the audience?

● Defining propaganda

Propaganda is a difficult term to define and labelling a documentary as propaganda is likely to provoke debate and disagreement. The use of film as propaganda is still most commonly associated with Nazi propaganda in the 1930s and 1940s (*Triumph of the Will* and *Olympia*, Leni Riefenstahl, both Germany, both 1935) and the study of the aims and techniques of these films can help in developing definitions of propaganda.

Nazi propaganda films fulfil the definitions of propaganda as:

- Possibly deceptive or distorted information spread systematically;
- Dissemination of information for the purpose of inducing or intensifying specific attitudes and actions;
- Information relying on an appeal to the emotions rather than the intellect.

One important aspect in the definition – and its distinction from other forms of political messages – is the emphasis on the systematic spread of information. To do this propaganda has to be produced by groups with power and the ability to reach a large proportion of the population (nationally and/or globally).

In practice this means that only some institutions have the position and power to produce and distribute propaganda:

- Political parties
- Mainstream religious groups
- Multinational corporations
- The state.

Propaganda also relies on an agreement within the institution – political party, church etc – about exactly what the message to be disseminated is. Propaganda relies on a central, authoritarian doctrine to be successful. It is for this reason that propaganda tends to be associated with dictatorships (eg Soviet propaganda) as democratic groups are often too diverse to have one central message.

The traditional definitions of propaganda have been affected by the development in the late 20th century of global conglomerates – multinational companies possessing great economic power and, arguably, influence. Global media companies owning film studios, television channels and newspapers across different countries are in an ideal position to disseminate information.

This idea is explored in the documentary *Outfoxed* (Robert Greenwald, US, 2004), which argues that the Fox news channel, a division of News Corporation, acts as a disseminator of propaganda rather than a news service.

Teaching tip

A study of *Outfoxed* is very useful in debating definitions of propaganda, opinion, subjectivity etc. It also draws on several other relevant areas for Film and Media Studies:

- News values
- Institution and ideology
- Manipulation of the audience
- Role of global companies in democracy.

While discussing the argument put forward by *Outfoxed*, students should also analyse the techniques of persuasion used by the documentary-makers themselves to convince the audience of their argument.

Central to the definition of propaganda is its systematic, organised and dogmatic nature, which distinguishes it from other important forms of political and social debate, such as social protest and campaigning.

● Social protest and campaigning documentary

Dennis De Nitto (1985) identifies the function of documentary as social commentary, ranging from the simple recording of social conditions to documentaries that attempt to bring about social and political change. De Nitto divides the social commentary film into three subgroups:

1. Social description
The films in this category present social conditions and reveal how people's lives are affected by institutions and environment. Criticism of these conditions is implied rather than explicit.

2. Social criticism
In this subgroup, the documentary-maker is less objective, pointing to problems in society in order to raise the audience's awareness.

3. Social protest
The most extreme group, this style of film foregrounds the anger of the filmmaker, who wants to provoke an active response from the audience.

This grouping of different types of social commentary can be helpful in analysing the different ways that documentaries have recorded, criticised and questioned society. It is likely that there will be some argument over allocating documentaries to these categories due to the range of different interpretations, eg for some people (Wells, 2000) the films of John Grierson fall into the category of social description, while Aitken's analysis (1997) suggests his work is an example of social criticism.

● The British documentary film movement

Key films

Drifters (John Grierson, UK, 1929)
Industrial Britain (Robert Flaherty, UK, 1931)
The Song of Ceylon (Basil Wright, UK, 1934)
Housing Problems (Arthur Elton, E H Anstey, UK, 1935)
Night Mail (Harry Watt and Basil Wright, UK, 1936)

Although these films are not all available on video/DVD, extracts and full versions are available online at: www.screenonline.co.uk and the Channel 4 website www.channel4.com/fourdocs/, both of which provide extensive resource materials.

Films from this period (late 1920s, early 1930s) have been used in this case study because they facilitate the discussion of:

● Documentary as part of a national cinema
● The link between documentary and the state
● Documentary and ideology.

The critical reputation of the British documentary movement has undergone great change since the 1930s. Initially the films were lauded but latterly, particularly since the 1970s, the work has often been attacked for its aims and techniques. It is therefore particularly important to have some understanding of the political and social context of Britain at the time as this directly affected the output of the movement.

Social and political context

The aims of the British documentary movement – and particularly its most influential contributor John Grierson – need to be placed in the wider society and political context of the 1920s and 1930s. This period in Britain is often characterised as one of instability and extremes, with large parts of the population affected by the Depression while a minority experienced great wealth and privilege. Against this background, the movements for popular democracy developed, including groups campaigning for equal rights to vote, an issue that had emerged at the end of World War I. The 1928 Reform Act meant that all men and women over the age of 21 were able to vote, no matter what their economic status was (the first Reform Act to widen the right to vote had been passed nearly 100 years before, in 1832).

In response to this, intellectuals and members of the establishment expressed concern about the effects of democracy: How could the uneducated masses be expected to make informed decisions about who to vote for? These ideas were particularly influential in the United States (where Grierson lived from 1924–7) where their main proponent was Walter Lippman (*Public Opinion*, 1922). These concerns were common not just among reactionaries, who felt that only the elite should be able to vote, but also among socialist thinkers. Grierson believed that he could educate the 'ordinary' people of Britain to help them become part of the democratic process and that this could be successfully done through film – the most powerful form of mass media.

John Grierson

Despite only directing one documentary (*Drifters*) – he was a film producer – Grierson is an important figure in the development of documentary. This is because his theories about the form have greatly influenced what we still understand to be its nature. Grierson defined documentary as an 'instrument of information, education and propaganda' and believed that it could be used to engage citizens in the workings of their country, in democracy. Given the instability of society in the 1920s and 1930s, Grierson saw documentary – and the mass media in general – as a tool for encouraging stability and cohesiveness. This could be done by emphasising and promoting the bond between the people and the state institutions; Grierson believed that citizens had a duty to serve the state, which in turn would look after them.

Grierson defined this ideology of social integration as 'good propaganda' while ideologies that promoted social division were 'propaganda of the devil' (Grierson in Aitken, 1997). An example of this in Grierson's view was the effect of unregulated capitalism, which meant that a small minority in society was amassing great wealth while the majority faced severe hardship. To counter this, the documentaries Grierson produced emphasised the importance of working-class communities in the successful running of the state, providing positive representations of social cohesion and integration. It is Grierson's belief in the importance of serving the state, but also in questioning the activities of some of the representatives of that state, which has meant that his documentaries can be defined as 'reformist and progressive' (Aitken, 1997) but also as examples of 'imperial propaganda' and 'domestic social engineering' (Winston, 1995).

Characteristics of the British documentary film movement

Probably the most famous definition of documentary is Grierson's description of it as 'the creative treatment of actuality', which distinguished it from newsreels and also suggested Grierson's interest in:

- The formal elements of documentary film as well as the social purpose
- The relationship between realism and representation.

Grierson is often accused of only being interested in documentary film as a vehicle for social comment and ideology rather than as an art form. In fact, the movement was characterised by its collaboration with artists, writers and composers associated with modernist and experimental movements in the arts: Benjamin Britten, J B Priestley, W H Auden. Many of the filmic techniques used, such as sound effects, music, montage editing and commentary (including the use of poetry in *Night Mail*) are modernist techniques and emphasise the 'creative' aspect of the documentary movement. It is also an example of Grierson's emphasis on co-operative working – sharing the filming, directing, editing etc – which did not suit all the members of the movement.

Throughout the 1930s Grierson worked for official and public sector film units which were set up to provide information about and promote the work of the state, these included:

Empire Marketing Board (EMB) Film Unit (1930–3)
In contemporary terms this could be described as providing spin or PR for the British Empire. Its aim was to promote the Empire as a benign, co-operative institution abroad. Directors working in the unit included Basil Wright, Arthur Elton, Harry Watt and Paul Rotha.

GPO Film Unit (1933–6)
With the closure of the EMB, the film unit transferred to the GPO and directors Humphrey Jennings and Alberto Cavalcanti joined. The most celebrated of the film units, this saw a prolific output of documentary films, but Grierson felt limited by the institution, leaving in 1936 to set up the Film Centre. Shortly afterwards, he left Britain to work for the National Film Board of Canada.

Crown Film Unit (1941–52)
At the beginning of World War II, the GPO Film Unit was taken over by the Ministry of Information and renamed the Crown Film Unit. It was responsible for wartime information and propaganda films.

There were also corporate film units in the same period such as those set up by Shell, Dunlop and ICI.

FOCUS FILM: *Night Mail*

Postal and train workers in Night Mail

Produced by Grierson at the GPO Film Unit, *Night Mail* records the mail train's journey from London to Glasgow. This journey provides the narrative structure of the film and the places it passes through are used to construct a particular representation of Britain. Linked to this is the representation of the postal and train workers. The film uses music by Benjamin Britten and the climax of the film includes the poem 'Night Mail', written and read by W H Auden.

Night Mail has been chosen as a close study film because of the way it challenges our expectations of what a documentary (particularly older examples) is through its use of formal experimentation, the latest technology and the reconstruction of particular scenes. It also uses propaganda techniques in a more oblique manner than students might expect and they need to analyse the way that a film about a train can also serve a political and social function. Although the film will seem very old-fashioned and dated to students, it is helpful to emphasise how modern the techniques and subject matter would have been in 1936.

Discussion points

- *Night Mail* uses a combination of realist and experimental techniques in its film language.
- There is a clearly identifiable narrative structure (the journey) which the real events are shaped to fit.
- Several scenes (the first dialogue scene, the mail sorters on the train) have been recreated in the studio rather than filmed as they happened, with much of the dialogue sounding 'scripted'.
- *Night Mail* doesn't fit neatly into any single documentary mode although it is usually defined as an expository documentary.
- *Night Mail* can be defined as an example of national cinema that represents British culture to a British audience. The British documentary movement was very influential in developing the realist style that characterises British cinema.
- *Night Mail* is an example of what John Grierson referred to as 'good propaganda', delivering a message of social cohesion where everyone – from all classes – works together for the good of the country.

Worksheet 7 *Night Mail* and film language

The approaches used in this worksheet could be used to construct an analysis of the whole film, but students could begin by focusing on the opening three minutes in detail. This worksheet asks students to identify the different types of film language used and to analyse how they contribute to the meaning and effect of the film.

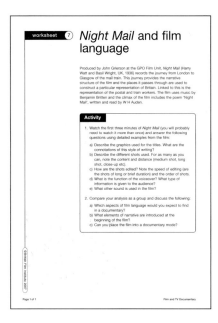

To access student worksheets and other online materials go to *Teaching Film and TV Documentary* at **www.bfi.org.uk/tfms** and enter User name: **docs@bfi.org.uk** and Password: **te1612do**.

- The graphics used for the title are typical of the modernist movement in the arts – clean, bold and streamlined – representing an optimistic view of the future based partly on a celebration of new technology.
- Editing is relatively rapid (fades and dissolves are also used throughout) and sometimes cuts abruptly from close-ups to long shots, creating rhythm and interest for the viewer.
- New techniques of aerial and trackside shots capture the speed of the train.
- The focus on the machinery and speed of the train – often in close-up – signals their importance and is part of a wider celebration of industry and technology.
- Music and sound effects are often used both to illustrate the images and to elicit an emotional response from the audience – a technique more commonly associated with fictional texts.
- The voiceover has a direct relationship to the images and is composed of detailed statistics and information about the train journey. The narrator speaks with received pronunciation (RP) identifying him as upper middle class. This accent was also characteristic of the BBC announcers at the period and for some critics typifies the patronising attitude of state institutions at that time.

Worksheet 8 *Night Mail* and the representation of Britain

This worksheet is intended for use with the whole film and asks students to analyse how the representation of people and places is constructed and the intended effect of these on the audience.

To access student worksheets and other online materials go to *Teaching Film and TV Documentary* at **www.bfi.org.uk/tfms** and enter User name: **docs@bfi.org.uk** and Password: **te1612do**.

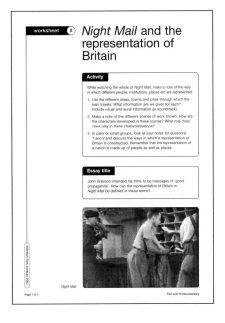

The film shows Britain and specifically England (note the newspaper headline about the Lords Test Match) as a traditional, agricultural country as well as an industrial one.

- The different regions and countries of Britain form part of the narrative of the film – the train's journey.
- Each area is given a character through the way it is filmed and the use of descriptive terms in the voiceover (this is also true of the train itself).
- Throughout the film the workers are shown to be dedicated and professional. They display character through their banter and humour as well as their age and experience. The men are continually shown to be working together and co-operating with each other; veterans teach the job to younger men and the management and workers show mutual respect.
- The representation of a mass of men working together to make sure the train runs on time is part of the central message of the film; the importance of social cohesion in creating a successful country.
- All the workers are men – the only women in the film are those serving tea at the station café.

Suggestions for further work

- Write a short (500 words) textual analysis of the representation of Britain in *Night Mail*.
- Think about how different and/or similar the subject matter of the film would be if it were set in Britain today.

- Use De Nitto's definitions to get students to debate the aims behind the film and whether or not it was successful.

● Humphrey Jennings and the poetic documentary

Humphrey Jennings' films were influenced by his interest in surrealist art as well as his Marxist sympathies and his films are usually seen as taking a very different approach to the work produced by Grierson. Jennings worked as part of, and was a founder member of, the Mass Observation Unit, a leftwing organisation engaged in an ambitious project of recording the lives of ordinary people in a variety of ways including on film. In his work, Jennings uses a poetic, rather than purely realist, and often surrealist style which combines the everyday events of people's lives with the extraordinary. According to Jennings, his films were neither propaganda nor ideological in purpose; instead he wanted to provoke an emotional response in the audience which would translate into concern for the plight of those depicted.

Teaching tip

One of Jennings' most celebrated films is *Listen to Britain* (UK, 1942 – available to watch at www.fourdocs.co.uk) which he described as a 'sound picture' rather than a documentary. Made for the Crown Film Unit, the aim of *Listen to Britain* was to heighten awareness in the US of the vulnerable position of Britain and to shift American public opinion into supporting their country's entry into the war. Although Grierson and Jennings are seen as taking different approaches to the documentary, it is interesting to compare this film with *Night Mail*. Students should consider the purpose of the two films, the representation of Britain and the use of film language; particularly techniques of voiceover, montage, sound effects.

Discussion point

How does the work of the British documentary movement affect our definitions of documentary? Consider the 'creative treatment of actuality', do the films studied show the 'real' world?

● Campaigning documentaries

The increased interest in and popularity of documentaries in recent years has in part been due to the development of polemical films that are often campaigning in purpose. The catalysts for this development were Michael Moore's films *Bowling for Columbine* (US, 2002) and *Fahrenheit 9/11*.

Teaching tip

As an introduction to this section it is helpful to review the definitions of propaganda in order to emphasise the distinction between campaigning documentaries and propaganda. It is quite easy for students to equate propaganda with subjectivity and therefore to define any biased or personal argument as propaganda. It is important therefore to stress the institutionalised and systematic nature of propaganda in comparison to the more independent and personal approach of the documentaries discussed here.

It is also helpful to place the documentaries in their wider social and cultural context. The one-sided nature of Morgan Spurlock's representation of McDonald's in *Super Size Me* has to be read through the audience's everyday experience of positive marketing by the company. Institutional context and audience are also important factors in looking at the films; nearly all are low budget, produced by independent companies. Although interest in documentaries has certainly increased, they are still seen by relatively few people at the cinema. (see www.imdb.com for information on budget and box office).

● Key films

Bowling for Columbine: Michael Moore argues that tragedies such as the Columbine massacre are a direct result of the gun laws in the US, which in turn can be linked to what he interprets as the country's aggressive foreign policy.

Fahrenheit 9/11: Developing some of the ideas from his previous film, Moore looks at the American response to 9/11 and how that shaped foreign and domestic policy. An extremely controversial film, great claims were made for its power of persuasion (eg *Buzz Around Moore's Movie May Be Able to Shake the Election*, Terry M. Neal, washingtonpost.com Friday, June 25, 2004) and it also provoked a great deal of anti-Moore criticism – both personal and professional.

Super Size Me: Produced at a time of wider concerns about the global domination of a few companies and the effect on society's health of eating too much fast food, *Super Size Me* uses a humorous, youth-orientated approach to attack McDonald's.

The Take (Avi Lewis, Canada, 2004), *The Corporation* (Mark Achbar and Jennifer Abbot, Canada, 2003), *Walmart: The High Cost of Low Price* (Robert Greenwald, US, 2005): These three documentaries attack global capitalism and examine its effect on the poor in societies across the world. *The Take* (written by Naomi Klein) follows the attempts by 30 car workers in Buenos Aires to take over their factory and restart production in the face of opposition from management and government. *Walmart* (by the director of *Outfoxed*) is an attack on the employment practices of the American chain and argues that it has destroyed independent retailers in the US and Europe. *The Corporation* (originally a TV series made for the Canadian Broadcasting Company, that country's equivalent of the BBC) takes an historical and psychological approach to argue that corporations – originally in the US but now globally – are constructed in such a way that they are only ever able to act in their own interests and therefore often to the detriment of everyone else.

An Inconvenient Truth: focuses on another contemporary issue – global warming – and follows Al Gore as he tours the US to educate people on the scientific background of global warming and attempts to get them to change their habits. A surprise commercial success, *An Inconvenient Truth* has (so far) taken $15m at the box office and was shown on 587 screens – an unusually high number for a documentary. (*The Great Global Warming Swindle*, Martin Durkin, Channel 4, 2007, and the controversy around its making and screening, would be an interesting area of comparison.)

Who Killed the Electric Car? (Chris Payne, US, 2006): This documentary also looks at environmental issues, specifically the West's reliance on the car and offers reasons for the lack of development of an alternative.

While the US and Canada dominate in the field of campaigning documentaries made for cinema exhibition, the UK has a similar tradition in television documentary. *Jamie's School Dinners* is a recent high-profile example of a campaigning series with a very clear aim: to improve the nutritional value of state school dinners.

Teaching tip

Jamie's School Dinners can be used in a variety of ways in teaching documentary:

- Analyse the documentary techniques in relation to different categories or modes.
- Define the series in terms of De Nitto's (1985) categories of social commentary.
- Discuss whether it is an example of propaganda, polemic, campaigning, investigative documentary etc.
- Use in conjunction with *Super Size Me* and/or *Walmart*. All three examples question the role of the commercial sector in public health policy as well as questioning capitalist ideology.
- Research the effect of the school dinners campaign through news archives and the related Channel 4 website – how successful has the series been in fulfilling its aims?
- Consider the role of Jamie Oliver as a celebrity in 'selling' the message of the film. How does his campaign fit with his sponsorship by Sainsbury's? What merchandising is available as a spin-off to the series?

Discussion point

What explanation is there for the rise in interest in campaigning documentaries on the part of both the filmmakers and the audience? Would you define the subject matter as political? Why do you think the makers of these films and programmes (who aren't all primarily documentary-makers) chose this way to publicise their cause?

● The investigative documentary

A related area in UK television is that of the investigative documentary, which is closely linked to journalism. The work of Brian Woods and Kate Blowett would provide an excellent area of research as their films link together social protest and investigation – most often concerned with human rights issues. Their most famous film *The Dying Rooms* (Channel 4, 1995) was an exposé of the conditions in Chinese orphanages. The Chinese authorities wanted the film banned and it led to an international outcry about human rights abuses. *The Dying Rooms* is available at: www.fourdocs.co.uk; due to the difficult subject matter the film won't be suitable for all students. Other films by Woods and Blowett include *Dying for Drugs* (Channel 4, 2003) about the pharmaceutical industry, *Kids behind Bars* (BBC, 2005), which looks at the lives of young offenders worldwide and *A World without Water* (Channel 4, 2006) about the role of the multinationals in the predicted global water shortage.

Discussion point

All the films referred to in the campaigning documentary section could be seen as dealing with broadly leftwing concerns (anti-capitalism, anti-globalisation, anti-corporate life etc), with some of the 'celebrities' involved such as Naomi Klein and Al Gore explicitly associated with Democrat politics. Can you think of any rightwing campaigning documentaries? What might these be concerned with? All of the films mentioned are low-budget independent productions. Why do you think this is?

FOCUS FILM: *Super Size Me*

Morgan Spurlock in Super Size Me

Super Size Me is one of the most commercially successful documentaries; it had an estimated budget of $300,000 and took $11.5m at the US box office, starting on 20 screens and being shown on 230 nine months later. (It is worth remembering the relative popularity of documentary; a Hollywood blockbuster is likely to be screened on 4000 screens in its first weekend.) It was also distributed across Europe. The success of the film in terms of its campaigning goal – to change the audience's eating habits – is much harder to determine.

The premise of the film is that Morgan Spurlock (the filmmaker) sets himself a challenge, to eat nothing but McDonald's food for 30 days and to monitor the effect of this on his body and emotions. The idea was apparently suggested by the failure of a court case brought against McDonald's by two obese girls who had argued that McDonald's food was responsible for their condition. *Super Size Me* is a participatory documentary featuring the filmmaker and is constructed – through subject matter and style – to appeal to a young audience not traditionally attracted to documentary.

Teaching tip

The approach developed for studying *Super Size Me* can be adapted to discuss any campaigning documentary. Key areas to investigate are:

- How does the film address the target audience?
- What techniques are used to keep the audience interested (suspense, obstacles, the character of the filmmaker, different film language etc)?
- What techniques are used to persuade the viewer about the truth of the argument?

Morgan Spurlock

Before watching the films, ask students to research Spurlock's career:

- What television programmes did he make before *Super Size Me*? Which institution were they made for? Are there any similarities in tone and style with *Super Size Me*?
- What projects has Spurlock developed since *Super Size Me*? This could include book and internet publishing as well as work for film and television.
- There are a lot of 'anti-Spurlock' sites on the internet. Who writes them and what do they accuse the filmmaker of?

Worksheets 9 and 10 *Super Size Me:* Film language, mode of address and persuasion

Worksheet 9 asks students to produce a textual analysis of the different film language and documentary techniques used and to consider the reasons for this style. Then students can discuss how the style is suitable for the audience and also how it is part of the film's persuasive technique.

To access student worksheets and
other online materials go to
Teaching Film and TV Documentary at
www.bfi.org.uk/tfms and enter
User name: **docs@bfi.org.uk** and
Password: **te1612do**.

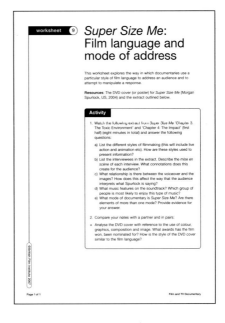

Film extracts: 'Chapter 3: The Toxic Environment' and 'Chapter 4: The Impact' (first half) (eight minutes in total).

Discussion points

- Titled sections break up the film, creating a narrative structure in relation to the number of days being marked. The emotive titles of these chapters are set against lurid paintings that satirise McDonald's iconography.

- Cartoons, computer graphics and various manipulations of the image are used in a style designed to appeal to younger audiences. These create a fast-paced backdrop for the amount of statistics presented.

- The montage of styles, rapid editing and loud soundtrack could be linked to the style of MTV – and addresses a similar audience. The central 'set-up' of the film and focus on bodily functions is also in the style of MTV programmes such as *Jackass*.

- The use of talking heads – experts who address an unseen interviewer and state their argument with authority – is typical of an expository documentary. Each expert interviewed is presented in a *mise en scène* to reinforce their expertise and knowledge (book-lined study, library, at a podium) making it difficult for the audience to question what they are saying.

- There is a direct link between the voiceover (by Spurlock) and the images shown, a technique that helps to reinforce the information given. The same technique is also employed in the interview with the Yale professor – as he outlines the increase in obesity in the US, the film cuts from him to images of fast food and overweight people. This is an example of the implicit argument that is constructed throughout the film; the professor doesn't say that McDonald's is responsible for the rise in obesity but the juxtaposition of his words and the filmmaker's images give that impression.

- In addition to the use of scientific experts, the voiceover employs a lot of statistics to present the argument.
- Observational and participatory techniques are also evident in the extract. The use of hand-held camera to film Spurlock's daily routine (having his food delivered, eating, meeting with his doctor) is an example of the observational style while Spurlock's speech to camera is participatory.
- *Super Size Me* is constructed through the integration of seemingly oppositional techniques. Some of the techniques present serious scientific knowledge based on fact but these are balanced by humour – in the soundtrack, the graphics and perhaps most importantly in the persona which Spurlock develops.

The style of *Super Size Me* is not only important in targeting the audience, it is also a very specific way of presenting and shaping an argument for that audience.

Worksheet 10 provides further context for the debate about the form and content of campaigning documentaries. Students are asked to read and discuss Omar Odeh, 'Jack-Ass II: Downsizing Morgan Spurlock's Super Size Me', available at: www.brightlightsfilm.com/45/supersizeme, which is very critical of the techniques used by Spurlock.

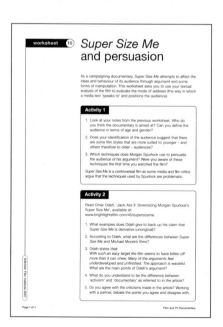

To access student worksheets and other online materials go to *Teaching Film and TV Documentary* at **www.bfi.org.uk/tfms** and enter User name: **docs@bfi.org.uk** and Password: **te1612do**.

Discussion point

What other style of documentary-making could be used to present the argument put forward in *Super Size Me*? Try to imagine the same information – health statistics, the global expansion of fast-food corporations and the progress of legal cases – presented in a more traditional mode of documentary such as a purely expository one. What would be the difference in the way the audience interprets the material? Would there be a different audience? Why did Spurlock choose to combine different types of documentary?

Argument and perspective

Nichols (1991) defines the different ways in which an argument is presented as perspective and it is the perspective that attempts to shape audience response. Spurlock's perspective relies to a great extent on the persona he constructs for the camera (as an audience we have no way of knowing whether he is like this off-camera), which is self-deprecating, humorous and sensitive. This persona has an ideological function which is carefully hidden: Spurlock is 'one of us', one of the good guys working against the anonymous, heartless fast-food corporations, thus taking part in a version of the David and Goliath story.

Fiction techniques

It is common to use narrative techniques associated with fiction in order to structure documentaries, for instance:

- The information may be presented as a journey that is followed from beginning to end (*Tracking Down Maggie*, Nick Broomfield, UK, 1994; *Roger and Me*, Michael Moore, US, 1989).
- The filmmaker will face a series of obstacles that they must overcome in order to complete their journey (the physical damage caused by eating too much fast food in *Super Size Me*, Courtney Love threatening the funding of the film in *Kurt and Courtney*).
- The obstacles create suspense for the audience, functioning in a similar way as in a detective story or thriller.
- The narrative structure creates a puzzle or enigma for the audience at the outset that it assumes will be resolved at the end.

Izod and Kilborn (1997) point out that it has now become a convention that the puzzle is not solved at the end; Michael Moore never does get to interview the head of General Motors, Nick Broomfield doesn't track down Thatcher (and only briefly intercepts Courtney Love). It is also the case that a meeting between the filmmaker and their subject is not actually likely to resolve any of the questions raised in the documentary – which suggests why it remains unfulfilled. For further discussion of the use of fictional techniques in documentary see Case study 3.

Suggestions for further work:

Fast Food Nation (Richard Linklater, US, 2006), an adaptation of the non-fiction book by Eric Schlosser, provides an alternative approach to Spurlock's as it is a fiction film based on real situations and events. Students could suggest some of the reasons for choosing the fiction form over documentary. The independent film production company behind *Fast Food Nation* is Participant Productions (set up by Jeff Skoll, one of the founders of eBay). This is an interesting institution to study as it produces documentaries and fiction films dealing with political and cultural issues. It states that:

> Participant believes in the power of the media to create great social change.

For more information go to: www.participantproductions.com.

Case study 2: Observational documentary and the new television formats

This case study traces the development of observational documentary in the 1960s to its contemporary influence on television formats such as docusoaps and reality television. This will include the study of the aims and form of observational filmmaking as well as the institutional context of contemporary formats.

● Defining observational documentary

While observational documentary is the particular mode of filmmaking, within that mode there are various movements that use the style in different ways.

● Direct cinema

> What if the filmmaker were simply to observe what happens in front of the camera without intervention? (Nichols, 2001)

Developed in the US in the 1960s, the key figures of this movement are the Maysles brothers, D A Pennebaker and Robert Drew and their aim was to challenge previous modes of documentary with the use of a new film language. They felt that traditional modes relied so heavily on manipulation in post-production that the reality of the events documented was lost. 'Direct' in this context refers to the relationship between the subject and representation – and the attempt to collapse the boundary between the two.

Key films

Primary (Robert Drew, US, 1960)
Gimme Shelter (Albert and David Maysles, US, 1970)
Salesman (Albert and David Maysles, US, 1969)
Don't Look Back (D A Pennebaker, US, 1967)
High School (Fred Wiseman, US, 1968)

- Non-intervention by the filmmaker, attempt to eradicate personal perspective.
- Emphasis on spontaneity, recording life as it is lived. This is often described as 'fly-on-the-wall' filmmaking.
- The documentary-maker is led by the subject rather than the other way round.
- The lack of intervention by the filmmaker means that the viewer has to become more active to understand the motivations and actions of the characters.
- The characters forming the focus of the documentary do not acknowledge that they are being filmed.
- Spontaneity is continued in post-production – no voiceover, non-diegetic music, special effects, reconstructions etc.
- Rather than issue-led films (social, political etc), direct cinema documentaries concerned individuals and their experiences.

Teaching tip

In discussing the aims of the direct cinema movement the debate can very quickly reach a dead end if the focus becomes too narrow in discussing whether or not documentary can be completely objective, without perspective or point of view. At the heart of observational filmmaking will always be the question:

- How does observing an event change it?

And the converse:

- How would the filmmaker's explicit presence change things?

The answer to this debate is ultimately unknowable; therefore it is more helpful to shift the focus to the more positive approach of:

- What is the role of the filmmaker in this mode and how does it differ from other areas studied?
- How does the observational technique allow us to see things that may otherwise have remained hidden?

● Albert Maysles

> Uncontrolled cinema, at least the way I practise it, I think requires a
> certain discipline to realise that it's so important not to intercede, not to
> take control – how do you expect to film reality if you try to control it?
> (Albert Maysles from *Albert Maysles, The Poetic Eye*, BBC4, 2006)

With his brother and main collaborator, David (who died in 1987), Albert
Maysles is an extremely influential documentary-maker, whose work, made for
American television in the 1960s, 1970s and 1980s, gained mass audiences.
One of the most celebrated examples was *Salesman* (US, 1969), which
followed the experiences of four door-to-door Bible salesmen as they
competed with each other to sign up customers. Shot in what is now seen as
a pure observational style – hand-held camera, natural lighting, very long takes
(which can make the documentary difficult to watch for contemporary
audiences) – the documentary was also innovative in its subject matter. While
workers had been the focus of documentary before (British documentary
movement in the 1930s), they were usually represented for ideological or
propaganda purposes. In focusing on the day-to-day experiences of a group
of people linked by their work, the Maysles brothers were attempting to record
the everyday lives of 'ordinary' people who would not usually have featured in
a documentary. The use of work as a structuring device in *Salesman* can be
seen as a forerunner of the docusoap.

Salesman is typical of the Maysles' early work and the direct cinema
movement in general, in that it is character- rather than issue-led; any social or
political issues evident are those developing from the characters' situation. In
Salesman, this was the issue of anti-Semitism. Maysles felt that issue
documentaries inevitably led to controlled and limiting filmmaking; the
documentary subject would always be contained within the filmmaker's
perspective and could never move outside it – the opposite of direct cinema's
wish to follow the subject wherever it went. Maysles, like Rouch (see below),
was a social scientist and believed that he had trained himself to study the
world objectively through his position as an observer. (In direct cinema,
confusingly, objectivity and observation become interchangeable.) Maysles
explains this scientific approach to documentary-making as 'noticing what
other people only watch' (*Albert Maysles, The Poetic Eye*, BBC4, 2006), a
statement which also alludes to the way that the camera records the world
('the poetic eye').

Despite Maysles' close association with direct cinema, his later films introduce
elements more usually associated with the participatory mode. In *Grey
Gardens* (Maysles brothers, US, 1975), the subjects of the documentary – an
eccentric elderly woman and her daughter, who are part of the American
aristocracy but live as near recluses – often address the documentary-maker

directly and refer to the presence of the crew. At one point the daughter says 'I want to show Al (Maysles) the photos'.

For more on Albert Maysles, go to www.mayslesfilms.com. This has material on direct cinema, past films and current projects. The work of the Maysles brothers is not easily accessible, although some films are available on Region 1 DVDs.

www.drewassociates.net is the website of Drew Associates – the direct cinema production company set up by Robert Drew, Richard Leacock and D A Pennebaker.

• Related movements

Cinéma vérité

Cinéma vérité is often used interchangeably with direct cinema but actually had very different aims – although the filmmakers involved did share techniques, collaborated on films and debated ideas about the nature of documentary. The term 'cinema truth' was first used by the French ethnologist and filmmaker, Jean Rouch, whose films were innovative in the use of new technology and in his approach to subject matter. The term was an homage to Vertov's (*Man with the Movie Camera*) Kino Pravda filmmaking – which strays very far from direct cinema's ideas about non-intervention. Instead Rouch, while using a film style very similar to observational documentary, was employing it for very different ends. Rouch's aim was to explore the reaction between the camera and subject, not to deny the camera's existence.

This is clear in *Chronicle of a Summer* (Jean Rouch and Edgar Morin, France, 1961). In the film, which was shot in the context of the end of the French war with Algeria, Rouch and Morin (a sociologist and filmmaker) investigate the nature of happiness by asking people in the streets of Paris whether or not they are happy. As the film progresses, the investigation becomes a way of finding out people's innermost thoughts about life and their relationship with others. The film is therefore based on the idea of intervention by the filmmakers, which was exactly what the direct cinema movement sought to avoid. Since the 1960s the term cinéma vérité has been used fairly loosely to describe any documentary that uses some observational techniques. This is because of the range of connotations attached to the term 'truth' in this context – Rouch meant the truth of the relationship between the subject and the camera, rather than the event which would happen whether or not the camera was there.

• Free cinema

A precursor of the observational mode of documentary was the British Free Cinema movement, developed in the mid-1950s by Lindsay Anderson, Tony Richardson and Karel Reisz. The Free Cinema movement did pioneer observational, location filming of 'pop culture' subjects (Margate funfair, a jazz club, a youth club) but its films were intended to be more poetic and impressionistic than the later observational cinema. This is evident in the use of montage and soundtracks (often jazz), influenced by the poetic films of Humphrey Jennings. For more on Free Cinema go to: www.bfi.org.uk/features/freecinema.

● Contemporary observational cinema

FOCUS FILM: *Être et Avoir*

George Lopez with schoolchildren

Être et Avoir is a good case study because it employs traditional observational documentary techniques (with some additions), which is unusual in contemporary documentary-making. It can also be used to discuss some of the ethical debates about this type of filmmaking (see below). Because it is an observational documentary (and a foreign-language film), students may find it difficult to watch. It is helpful therefore to prepare students for the kind of film it is, to have precisely focused activities and to emphasise the link between the form and content.

Discussion points

It is also important to draw attention to the way that observational documentaries can be read – and used – ideologically. While the aim of campaigning documentaries is explicit, the representation constructed in observational documentary can also be influential. The film's director, Nicholas

Philibert, has stated that he did not want the film to be didactic (see the director's statement on the film's official website, link from www.bbc.co.uk/bbcfour/documentaries/storyville/) but in France it has been used politically. As the type of school which *Être et Avoir* features disappears, the film has been used by some to argue for the need to keep and support this tradition. For the supporters of this type of school, the film celebrates a traditional, rural French way of life that is seen in opposition to the values of contemporary city life. It is this reading of the film which has also led to accusations of nostalgia, that it presents a rose-tinted view of this particular way of life. The debate over the meaning of the film illustrates the way that different audiences can have different interpretations. This is also evident in the reaction to the representation of Georges Lopez, the teacher. Some students are likely to see him as a kind and benevolent man, while others view him as authoritarian, old-fashioned and at times unfeeling.

Être et Avoir has also been the centre of a legal dispute. Georges Lopez, the teacher featured in the film, sued the film director for a share of the profits. For the background to this legal dispute see: Amelia Gentleman, 'Defeat for teacher who sued over film profits', 29/09/04, available at: www.//film.guardian.co.uk/print/0,,5026776-3156,00.html. For a discussion of the wider issues in relation to documentary-making, see Mark Lawson, 'Whose Life Is It Anyway?' at: www.buzzle.com/editorials/10-11-2003-46396.asp.

Worksheets 11 and 12 *Être et Avoir*: Film language and narrative structure

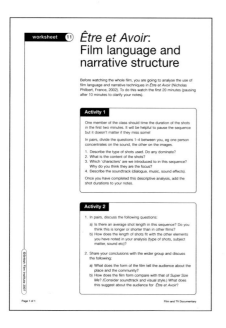

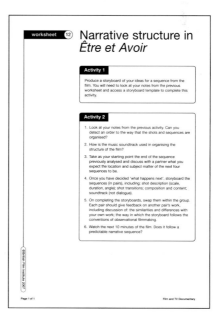

Film extract: The opening of the film (20 minutes, to be shown in two sections)

These worksheets provide a framework for students to construct an analysis of the film language, to analyse the link between form and content and to discuss the mode of address. Examining the way in which the director has structured the footage into a narrative, the worksheet asks the students to storyboard a sequence.

Points to note

- The use of long takes, static shots with minimal action.
- In the classroom the camera tends to be positioned at the students' eye level, meaning that the teacher is often out of frame.
- Lack of exposition: unlike other modes of documentary there is no voiceover to explain what is happening, who the people are etc.
- The film is very quiet but with non-diegetic, classical music used during shots of the countryside.
- The slow pace of the film reflects the way of life in the community.
- The structure of this extract sets up the organisation of the film as a whole: the overarching structure of the seasons (beginning in autumn/winter), the school day, and the microstructure of the order of the shots; the countryside, the classroom, the countryside, students' home lives and so on.
- Characterisation: the schoolteacher and certain students are chosen as the focus of the film, creating a specific representation of the school and the village and a source of identification for the audience.
- The mode of address signifies a serious and traditional perspective aimed at an older audience (and in the UK, one which watches foreign-language films).

● Criticisms of direct and observational cinema

Direct cinema – and observational cinema in general – has been a controversial form with criticisms directed at its aim of recording unmediated reality as well as ethical questions about the style. Documentary-maker Errol Morris (1993, in Bruzzi, 2000) stated that the observational style had set back the development of documentary form because audiences equated the observational style with truth, therefore viewing other modes as somehow 'fake'.

● Realism and observational techniques

One of the main elements of direct cinema style was to make the audience feel involved in the actions on screen, to feel as if these events were taking place in the present. To be able to do this, viewers couldn't be reminded that what they were watching had been filmed, recorded and edited. Therefore the aim was to make the film language invisible. This is a similar idea to the audience's suspension of disbelief in Hollywood cinema; if we are reminded that we are watching a film we may lose the ability to believe in what we see on screen. The different modes of interactive documentary-making specifically attacked this approach by foregrounding the process of filmmaking so that the audience is always aware of the process of filmmaking. Despite these different approaches, it is important to remember that observational techniques are still used a great deal in documentaries that would be termed participatory or performative.

● Observational cinema and ethical questions

The controversy about observational cinema also concerns the effect on the subjects – or social actors – of being part of a documentary and watched by a mass audience. This is an issue given renewed relevance with the rise of the docusoap and reality television.

These concerns can be summarised as the following:

- Is the observational mode inherently voyeuristic? If so what is the effect on the subjects of this 'through-the-keyhole' relationship?
- In addition to the effect on the subject, what does the voyeuristic impulse suggest about the audience? Does it have an affect on audience behaviour outside of watching the programme?
- How and why are subjects chosen? Are choices ever driven by the pressure on documentary-makers to provide titillation for the audience (and ratings for the institution)?
- What consideration is given to the long-term consequences for participants in the documentary? How thorough is the discussion of consent? If the social actors are children, how will they feel in the future? The ongoing documentary series *7 Up* (Granada, UK, 1964–present), which traces the changes in children's lives in Britain, provides some indication of the pressures of appearing in a documentary, with several of the participants declining to take part in later films. Maysles has discussed how he treats his subjects with 'love' and 'respect' and that trust between the filmmaker and subject is essential. He has also remained in touch with many of the subjects of his films, but it is debatable how true this is of other filmmakers and producers.
- Should the filmmaker ever intervene in the actions they are observing or allow them to play out as if they weren't there? What if a participant is going to hurt himself or someone else? What if the filmmaker discovers information that should be given to the police? (In *Paradise Lost: The Child Murders at Robin Hood Hills* (Joe Berlinger and Bruce Sinofsky, US, 1996), the stepfather of one of the murdered children gives the filmmakers a knife which they give to the police. The knife is then used in evidence at the trial.)

While charges of exploitation and voyeurism have always been aimed at observational documentary, they have become foregrounded with the popularity of its descendants the docusoap and reality television.

● Popular factual programming

Corner (2000) defined four phases in the recent development of popular factual programming:

- Reality television
- Docusoap
- Docushow
- The reality game show.

Reality television (peak of popularity late 1980s to mid-1990s)

Originating in the US, this phase of reality television used techniques from documentary – hand-held camera, location shooting, direct sound recording – with reconstructions, dramatic music and emotive voiceover. The focus of the first reality programmes were the institutions of law and order – particularly the police – crime and the emergency services; subjects which provide dramatic, emotional and often violent scenes. The most influential of these shows was *Cops* (Fox, 1989–present), which was copied internationally (*Blues and Twos*, Carlton, 1993; *Coppers*, Sky One, 1994) and is still shown on Saturday night primetime on Fox. The BBC created *999 Lifesavers* (1994), which followed the format of the US shows but also added advice on first aid and life-saving – in keeping with its public service remit.

Docusoap (mid-1990s to 2000)

The docusoap form adopted elements of reality television, particularly the emphasis on ordinary people's experiences linked by a particular job or institution, but placed it in a family-friendly context (often to do with animals and caring). *Animal Hospital* (BBC1, 1985–2004) proved the viability of docusoaps in terms of ratings; scheduled against *The Bill* (ITV, 1994–present) it gained a substantial audience share. The docusoap is discussed in more detail below.

Docushow (late 1990s–present)

The docushow is a presenter-led programme that often deals with lifestyle – gardening, the home, fashion, beauty, health etc. This format focuses on the experience of real people to illustrate different aspects of the chosen theme: buying a house, going on a diet, having plastic surgery or creating a new garden. As the style has developed, the programmes have become more emotional. The concept of a psychological makeover has become central to the programme message, suggesting that, for example, a new set of clothes can affect a person's life in a profound way. Examples include: *What Not to Wear* (BBC, 2002–present), *Location, Location, Location* (Channel 4, 2001–present) *You Are What You Eat* (Channel 4, 2004–present), *Ten Years Younger* (Channel 4, 2004–present).

The reality game show (*now more usually referred to as reality television*) (*2000–present*)

This phase borrows elements from the previous reality phase and the docusoap, placing ordinary people (although carefully selected by the producers) within a specifically constructed context. Therefore the convention that had remained from observational documentary of the 1960s, observing people within their natural environment, had gone. The other major development has been the introduction of a competitive element from the game show genre, which is more or less dominant depending on the programme.

● The docusoap

The docusoap, which reached the height of its popularity in the 1980s and 1990s, exhibits the most obvious links to the work of Direct cinema in the 1960s. The similarities include:

● Fly-on-the-wall filming techniques.
● Emphasis on spontaneity; events happening in the present.
● Interest in relationships and emotions rather than wider issues.

There are also clear differences between the styles:

● Exaggerated or 'hyperbolic' (Winston, 1999) characters. These include Maureen in *Driving School* (BBC, 1997) who keeps failing her driving test, the parking attendant who gives out hundreds of tickets in *Clampers* (BBC1, 1998), the veterinary student who fails her final exams in *Vet School* (ITV, !993–4), the tough hotel manager in *Hotel* (BBC, 1997). The exaggeration also extends to characteristics: social actors with clearly identifiable appearances and mannerisms became central to a programme's success.
● The docusoap is a series rather than a single film. One of the first docusoaps (or fly-on-the-wall documentary series as it was referred to at the time), *The Family* (BBC, 1974) ran for just 12 30-minute episodes. Now a docusoap is a long-running, returning series.
● Direct cinema was an auteur movement; in the docusoap, genre is dominant.
● Soap opera conventions are common, such as melodramatic storylines and cliffhangers; short scenes; multiple narrative strands and characters; and a variety of tone and duration of storylines.

The docusoap was an extremely popular form. While all the terrestrial channels developed their own series, it was a genre particularly associated with the BBC. The docusoap was particularly important to the BBC because it fulfilled its remit as a public service broadcaster (having its roots in documentary, the genre was defended as educational) and was a ratings success (the most popular docusoaps gained between 40% and 50% of audience share for specific episodes during the early to mid-1990s). It was also cost-effective with episodes of docusoap budgeted at an average of £65,000, roughly one-fifth of the budget for drama. The genre was also suitable for the new multichannel era.

The series *Airport* (BBC, 1997), set in London's Heathrow airport is a good example of this.

- It began on BBC2 in 1996, but the popularity of some of the recurring characters (particularly Jeremy Spake, the Aeroflot employee) led to a move to BBC1 and a primetime slot where it often gained 12 million viewers.
- Jeremy Spake became a BBC 'star' and was under contract as a presenter on various light entertainment programmes.
- The series was shown in Australia, Canada and South Africa. Later it was sold to the satellite channel UKTV.
- Special editions of *Airport* from around the world were shown between series and a live edition was also shown on BBC daytime.
- BBC1 regularly repeats the series; UKTV still shows *Airport* daily and also has special *Airport* weekends where episodes are shown throughout the day.
- The most recent series was in 2005.

Worksheet 14 Defining the docusoap

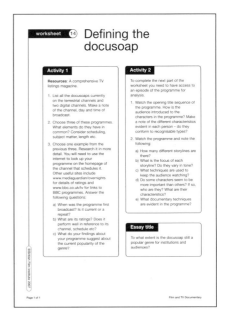

To access student worksheets and other online materials go to *Teaching Film and TV Documentary* at **www.bfi.org.uk/tfms** and enter User name: **docs@bfi.org.uk** and Password: **te1612do**.

This worksheet is based on textual analysis, addressing the way that the docusoap uses conventions from the soap opera and documentary. (This approach could also be used as an extension of the study of soap opera – such as in Med 2, AQA). The worksheet activity can be used with any example of the docusoap – it is suggested that students research and analyse a programme of their own choice.

Reasons for the decline in popularity

The docusoap became an increasingly controversial form in the 1990s, coming in for a number of different criticisms.

These included:

- Accusations of reconstruction and 'fakery'. The most prominent example of this was the admission by the producers of *Driving School* that some of the scenes had been reconstructed eg Maureen supposedly practising for her test at 4am was actually filmed later in the day.
- The increasing number of docusoap series, particularly on the BBC, led to accusations of 'dumbing down' as the series were made more cheaply, focused on increasingly banal subjects and became, to some commentators, voyeuristic.
- The docusoap was seen to represent a decline in the documentary genre from the golden age of the 1960s.

For an example of the type of criticisms made against the docusoap, see B Winston (1999), 'The Primrose Path: Faking UK Television Documentary, Docuglitz and Docusoap', *Screening the Past* available at: www.latrobe.edu.au/screeningthepast/firstrelease/fr1199/bwfr8b.htm.

Discussion point

The above criticisms raise various issues about the nature of documentary. The first reveals how entrenched the idea of documentary as unmediated reality is. Is the faking of scenes in documentary wrong? What is the difference between a fake scene and a reconstruction? Is there a difference between reshooting a scene that did happen and inventing one?

There was a very excitable media response at the time which also included accusations that the talk show *Vanessa* (ITV, 1994) planted people in the studio audience to instigate a more extreme reaction.

The second area of criticism – the accusation of dumbing down – is a familiar argument in the context of public service broadcasting where institutions are easily attacked for being too elitist or too broad. The BBC responded to criticism by announcing in 2001 an end of the dominance of the format and a move to a more varied schedule (see Nick Higham, 'The End of Reality TV', BBC News Online, 22/05/01).

Related to the public service broadcast debate is the attack on the docusoap style with some critics seeing it as a corruption of the documentary itself.

> Here are documentaries made in exploitative and unethical ways about nothing in particular, which overtly and obviously encourage the people involved to overact in a largely uncharacteristic and often sensationalist way. (Winston, 1999)

In response to this analysis, it could be argued that the docusoap witnessed the first time that documentary had appealed to a mass working-class audience – who were also represented on screen – since the 1930s.

Docusoap can also be problematic for institutions. In 2000, the BBC had to pay libel damages to a woman who had been shown being asked to leave the Adelphi Hotel in *Hotel* because she was (wrongly) suspected of being a prostitute. In 2004, a woman was sentenced to 12 months' community service for creating a bomb scare at Luton airport, the subject of *Airline*. The prosecution at her trial stated:

> It became plain once Mrs. Brennan was aware the cameras were focusing on her, she rather played up to them.

End of the docusoap?

- Despite the BBC's announcement of the end of its reliance on docusoaps, they still form part of the broadcaster's schedule (terrestrial, freeview, satellite).
- The genre has been developed and adapted to create new hybrid styles in daytime and primetime programming – *Escape to the Country* (BBC2, 2002–present), *City Hospital*, *Traffic Cops*, *A Life of Grime* (all BBC1, 1998–present), *A Year at Kew*, *A Seaside Parish* (both BBC2, 2004–present), *The House of Tiny Tearaways* (2005–present), *Honey We're Killing the Kids* (both BBC3, 2005–present)
- It has been argued that the docusoap has been subsumed by reality television and the BBC has had (varied) success with programmes in this area: *Castaway* (BBC1, 2000), *Fame Academy* (BBC1, 2002), *The Convent* (BBC2, 2006), *The Apprentice* (BBC2, 2005), *Dragon's Den* (BBC2, 2006). The BBC's association with reality television led to similar accusations of dumbing down as with the earlier docusoap.

Worksheet 15 Popular factual programming and hybrid genres

Students are asked to analyse the extent to which contemporary factual programming mixes observational techniques, the docusoap, reality television, the game show and light entertainment formats. For this worksheet, students need to watch a range of examples from different formats and institutions.

To access student worksheets and other online materials go to *Teaching Film and TV Documentary* at **www.bfi.org.uk/tfms** and enter User name: **docs@bfi.org.uk** and Password: **te1612do**.

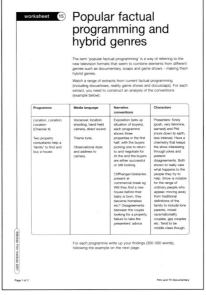

1 of 2 pages

● Reality television and *Big Brother*

Big Brother is the most successful and controversial example of reality television in Britain (and internationally). It is a useful case study as students often have a great deal of knowledge and understanding of the series as viewers of the programme.

It also provides an opportunity to discuss some of the key debates in media (essential for many A2 Media Studies specifications):

● Convergence and new technologies
● Globalisation
● Representation.

Media convergence

The concept of media convergence is now a reality for many members of the audience, with the youth audience being the initial target (see Chris Tryhorn (2005), 'Ofcom Confirms Old Media Fears' available at: www.mediaguardian. co.uk/broadcast). Convergence is an economic strategy which sees media institutions attempt to minimise the gap between the different media and technological platforms that they own. In other words, it is an attempt to gain profit by making a range of media companies work together ie digital and satellite television and film channels, DVD, mobile phones, internet and broadband, personal computers. The ultimate ideal would be for the consumer (audience member) to be able to use one piece of technology (a PC, a mobile phone etc) for all their media needs (watching television, internet surfing, listening to radio programmes, downloading music and films, making telephone calls, taking photos etc).

The current strategy of media convergence has been made possible by four developments:

1. Multimedia, global conglomerates: the global media are increasingly owned by a handful of companies – sometimes referred to as the 'Big 6' (News Corporation, the Walt Disney Company, Viacom, Sony, Time Warner, NBC Universal).
2. Digitisation: media content is produced in a universal computer language that can easily be adapted for use across different media.
3. Government deregulation: this has meant that conglomerates have been allowed to own different kinds of media in the same market. For example, in the UK, News International owns BSkyB (satellite television and broadband) as well as newspapers *The Times* and *The Sun*.
4. Rapid take-up of home technology: broadband technology has been the fastest-growing new technology and is the crucial element in the practical application of convergence. In the UK, by September 2005, take-up was 7.8 million subscribers which is a 30% penetration (September 2005 figures from Department of Trade and Industry report available at: www.broadbanduk.org/reports/dti which will also have updated figures).

The benefits of convergence for conglomerates can be immense:

● Reduction of production (and administration and personnel) costs as the same content is used across media.
● Increased advertising opportunities and revenue (advertisers can be sold cross-media packages); this is particularly important with the rise in ownership of systems such as Sky Plus and TIVO which allow viewers to skip traditional adverts.
● Increased brand recognition and audience loyalty through cross-promotion and selling.

Convergence is also a controversial development in media because:

● It reinforces the power of the large conglomerates, making it more difficult for new producers to enter the media and reducing competition.
● The content (film, television, newspaper etc) becomes just another product; qualities such as creativity and originality could become of secondary importance to the opportunities it provides for convergence.
● It is another example of globalisation – convergence is likely to mean the reliance on a few formats that can be watched by a global audience, rather than the distinctive and different qualities of national media products.

Examples of convergent media

Google

The internet search engine now offers the chance to download videos, news reports, films and television series. Some of these are free but others (eg the Sundance channel and series such as *CSI*) are charged for, either on a pay-per-view or 'season ticket' system.

The Guardian

The Guardian is the leading newspaper for utilising new technology; it had one of the first and most comprehensive websites and its relaunch in the 'Berliner' format was made economically possible by new digital technology. The example of *The Guardian* is particularly useful in helping students to understand the nature of convergence – the print version of the newspaper and the internet version are literally converging, becoming the same thing through digital technology.

Teaching tip

Ask students to produce a list of the different ways that you can access *The Guardian*.

- Print-based newspaper – on sale at newsagents, supermarkets etc.
- Website, which then offers further means to access the 'newspaper': News can be sent to a mobile phone, email or desktop. You can print your own PDF version (GD4), which can be continually updated. There are digital editions (also of *The Observer*) that recreate the experience of reading the print-based paper. (You can browse the demo on the main website.)

Once students have completed an analysis of the website, they could look at the print-based edition and note the different ways that that version refers to and promotes the internet site.

Discussion point

Will traditional print-based newspapers exist in two years' time? In five or ten years' time? What do students think are the advantages of internet newspapers compared to print-based editions? (It is useful to think about interactivity and reader choice here – suggestions that digital newspapers are more portable is problematic.) What might be some of the disadvantages? What happens to people (not just the old) who don't have easy access to new technology?

Channel 4, Big Brother *and convergence*

The success – and controversy – of *Big Brother* is in part due to the use of convergence. *Big Brother* was the first series shown on British television to fully exploit new technologies to build brand awareness and create revenue opportunities beyond the traditional means of advertising. In this instance Channel 4 has been in the forefront of technological convergence, moving away from traditional forms of television exhibition.

The Channel 4 website currently offers the opportunity to watch episodes of the series *Lost* online as well as the chance to download podcasts from the newly launched Channel 4 radio programmes to an mp3 player. Channel 4 signed a deal with Endemol (the inventors of the format) to broadcast *Big Brother* until 2007. It is rumoured that ITV will bid for the rights for the following year, having had limited success with their own reality formats.

Channel 4 is a publicly owned corporation whose board is appointed by Ofcom, the television regulator. Channel 4 does not receive public funding but makes profit through its own commercial activities. The corporation is typical of contemporary television institutions in that it is a publisher/broadcaster; it does not produce its own programme content but commissions it from national and international companies.

4Ventures is the Channel 4 subsidiary company which, according to the Channel 4 website:

> carries the channel's values and audiences into the multi channel, multi platform future (www.channel4.com/about_Channel 4)

and *Big Brother* has been a crucial part of this strategy.

● Endemol

Channel 4 buys the *Big Brother* programme and brand from Endemol, a Dutch owned production company. Some research in to Endemol (www.endemol.com) raises interesting questions about the future of British television in the context of global media formats.

Worksheets 16 and **17 Case study of *Big Brother***

These worksheets ask students to analyse Endemol's aims and the way in which these are developed through the selling of formats. Students can then link their findings to the way in which Channel 4 exploits the *Big Brother* brand.

- Endemol's top 10 formats are all reality television, game-show hybrids, which can be easily adapted to different markets and offer opportunities for audience interactivity.
- These formats are sold to 25 countries globally – it operates like a franchise.
- Endemol sells itself on its ability to take the problems out of programming and scheduling by setting up the series.
- The promo on participation television emphasises television programming as an economic product used to make a profit.

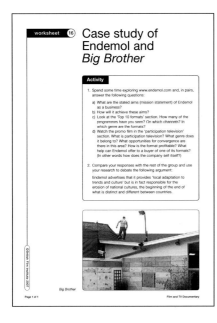

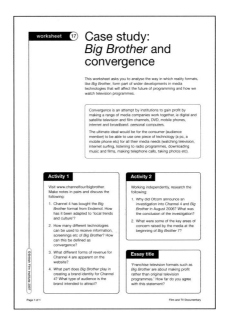

The Endemol business model is an influential one, as can be seen in the example of *Strictly Come Dancing* (BBC1, 2004–present). The BBC has now sold the format (rather than the BBC series) to Europe and the US.

- *Big Brother* was sponsored by Carphone Warehouse which, in addition to selling mobile phones, now operates as an internet service provider (ISP). (Carphone Warehouse withdrew its sponsorship due to the accusations of racism in *Celebrity Big Brother* (2007), suggesting some risks for brands in associating with controversial programmes.)
- *Big Brother* is 'live' – on television (E4) and online. Online access is £1.99 per day or £3.99 per week.
- In addition to the live stream, podcasts of highlights are available to download onto an mp3 player.
- News updates about *Big Brother* can be sent by text message or direct to your desktop.
- You can download ringtones and wallpaper to your mobile, purchase clothes and accessories from the online shop.
- The largest area of revenue for the channel is the voting (which can't be done on the website); premium rate phone call 50p plus standard text rate from a mobile.
- There are *Big Brother* shows on Channel 4, E4 and More4, developing coverage of the brand and raising the profile of the corporation's digital channels.
- The spin-off shows are interactive participation programmes, relying on the audience to text in their views.

- These shows also work as a training ground for new Channel 4 personalities, who will be associated with the brand, such as Russell Brand.
- The links from the website include one to an online betting service, which is another example of an industry which has been transformed by online services. It also raises questions about the audience for this website (Channel 4 argues that the online 'pay' service is aimed at those aged 18 years and above – although there is no regulation of this).
  See www.channel4.com/bigbrother.

● Convergence and regulation

The content of television is regulated by Ofcom, which in turn administers government legislation. The output of online services has not yet been regulated although the 2003 Communications Act left open the possibility of extending TV regulations to online services. This became more pertinent recently when an alleged sexual assault on *Big Brother* in Australia was shown on the live internet stream. Channel 4's internet stream is actually the same as that shown on E4 and has a 15-minute delay to avoid such a situation.

The question of regulatory control of internet output is an important one. Sweney (2006) defines two key tests which could determine whether a website can be regulated like television:

- Is it available to be viewed by the general public in the same way that television is? (Pay-on-demand services like those on the *Big Brother* website fall outside this definition.)
- Is the primary purpose of the website to deliver audiovisual material? (In the case of the *Big Brother* website it is part of Channel 4 webpages which provide a variety of content, not all audiovisual.)

Suggestions for further work

Use the online streaming or footage on E4 to define the conventions of observational documentary. How close is the relationship between representation and reality in these programmes?

Big Brother would be a good case study for issues of representation with reference to stereotyping, gender, sexuality, regional identity, disability etc. See Rebecca Atkinson (2006), 'When Will Soaps Follow Big Brother's Lead?' available at: www://media.guardian.co.uk/bigbrother/story/ for a discussion of the representation of disability.

What is the future of reality television? Will audiences tire of the format? Is the potential of convergence too great for institutions to drop the formats?

In 2005, it was announced that the BBC was looking for families to take part in a year-long reality show (a real-life *EastEnders*). What has happened to this project?

Case study 3: Documentary and performance

● Director as star and drama-documentary

This case study looks at the recent developments in the documentary form, which question the validity of traditional documentary modes and which increasingly blur the boundaries between fact and fiction.

● The performative documentary

As previously mentioned, the definition of performative documentary is debatable and it is closely linked to participatory and reflexive modes. It is helpful to think of the performative mode in three broad subcategories:

1. Those that experiment with form so that the film language itself becomes a type of performance, rather than just in service to the subject matter.
2. Those that have the theme of performance as their subject matter. This definition initially developed from feminist and postmodern theorists who were interested in the idea of gender as a performance. *Paris Is Burning* (Jennie Livingston, US, 1990) is the key film in this definition. Set in New York, it follows the lives of people who perform in drag and take part in drag balls. The documentary raises issues of gender expectations and questions to what extent these characteristics are natural or performed. (*Paris Is Burning* is discussed in Butler (1993) and Flinn (1998).) It is not necessarily the case that a documentary about performance will also be a performative documentary but Bruzzi (2000) cites *Geri* (Molly Dineen, UK, 2001) as an example of a film that has performance as its subject matter (the 'performance' which Geri Halliwell gives as Ginger Spice) and is also a performative documentary.
3. Those where the performance of the documentary-maker is the central focus of the film, drawing the audience's attention to the way that the documentary is constructed. This type of performative documentary also raises questions about authorship in documentary, featuring the director as 'star' (Nick Broomfield, Michael Moore and on television, Molly Dineen, Louis Theroux, Jon Ronson etc).

This case study focuses on this aspect of the performative mode.

● Conventions of the performative mode

● The filmmaker appears on screen and it is their interaction (or lack of) with the subject that is often the central focus.
● The voiceover is by the filmmaker, emphasising their feelings and reactions to events.
● Interviews dominate the form, sometimes arranged and relatively formal but often done 'on the run', taking the interviewee by surprise.

- The narrative structure of a journey or investigation (which may not reach a conclusion) is used.
- The style is characterised by a seemingly amateur aesthetic: shaky camera, poor sound quality, uncertainty on the part of the interviewees and interviewer.
- There is an emphasis on the problems of making the documentary – raising money, arranging interviews, problems with equipment – which is hidden in other modes of documentary.
- The apparent subject of the documentary is often marginalised – or never appears.
- Peripheral characters in the documentary become central as the original subject becomes less important.

The performative mode – to a greater extent than other forms – is marketed on the basis of the director; 'A Nick Broomfield film' etc in a similar way to a director of fiction films. The prominence of the director is one of the reasons for controversy in this area. For further discussion of the conventions of this mode of documentary, see Ronson (2002), who discusses the work of Michael Moore from the perspective of being a documentary-maker himself.

FOCUS FILMS: *Kurt and Courtney* (1998) and *Aileen: Life and Death of a Serial Killer* (2003) (both Nick Broomfield, both UK)

Both of these films – despite their differences – fulfil the conventions of the performative documentary and foreground questions about the role of the documentary-maker.

- *Kurt and Courtney* (1998)

Kurt and Courtney

Courtney Love

After the death of Kurt Cobain (the lead singer with Nirvana), Nick Broomfield began a film about the relationship between Kurt and his wife Courtney Love and the seemingly mysterious circumstances of the singer's death. While this is the starting point, the film actually follows many different stories and characters – often those on the margins of society – in a way that is typical of Broomfield's work.

Discussion points

- Documentary conventions. The film language is typical of a performative documentary (hand-held camera, predominance of interviews, voiceover etc).
- Narrative structure. The investigation.
- Manipulation of audience response. Throughout the documentary, the interviewees selected are far more sympathetic to Kurt than Courtney. The filming and presentation of the interviewees is also important in constructing a particular audience response.
- The documentary-maker as subjective. Nick Broomfield appears to be developing a feud with Courtney Love which suggests his reactions to the story are no longer objective.
- The director as star. Nick Broomfield appears throughout the film interacting with people and even altering events by intervention. At the end of the film he appears – uninvited – onstage at an awards ceremony attended by Courtney Love to make a speech accusing her of censorship.
- The foregrounding of the process of documentary-making. This includes problems with funding and the difficulty of interviewing Courtney Love.
- Authorship theory. In addition to being typical of Broomfield's film style, the themes explored in *Kurt and Courtney* also recur across his work. These include the nature of celebrity, the effects of fame on individuals and an evident sympathy with people who don't fit into mainstream society.

• Aileen: Life and Death of a Serial Killer

Aileen Wuornos murdered seven men while working as a prostitute in the southern states of the US. She was subsequently tried and sentenced to death. *Aileen: Life and Death of a Serial Killer* is Broomfield's second film about Wournos (the first *Aileen Wuornos:The Selling of a Serial Killer*, made in 1992, covered her original trial) and follows her from her final appeal to execution. This documentary has been chosen as a case study because in addition to the debates it raises about the performative mode, it also leads to discussion of wider themes. Wuornos's story is told in order to attack the US legal system and the death penalty. It is a demanding, and at times disturbing, documentary but one which engages students and asks them to examine their ideas on contemporary issues, particularly that of social inequality.

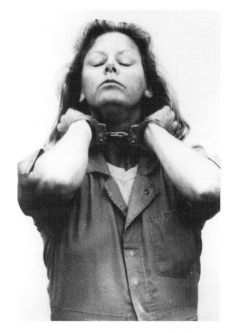

Aileen Wuornos in Aileen: Life and Death of a Serial Killer

Discussion points

- The similarity to the conventions used in *Kurt and Courtney.*
- The catalyst for the making of the documentary is Broomfield being subpoenaed to appear as a witness at Wuornos's appeal, making the documentary-maker part of the subject.
- The documentary constructs an image of Wuornos which persuades the audience to see her as a victim – as well as a murderer.
- Broomfield appears to have an emotional response to Wournos and is obviously affected by what happens to her, rather than remaining detached.
- In a similar scene to the awards ceremony in *Kurt and Courtney*, Broomfield makes a speech to the US media attacking the death penalty at the time of Wournos's execution.

Teaching tip

Students may be familiar with the subject matter as Wuornos's life story was the focus of *Monster* (Patty Jenkins, US, 2003) and it would be interesting to analyse the different ways in which fiction and documentary construct audience response – sympathy, identification with characters etc.

● The director as star: Authorship and documentary

This definition of performative documentary draws on wider concepts in film theory – authorship and star studies (sometimes now referred to as performance studies) and it is helpful to use some elements from these approaches as context for further study of individual examples.

Nick Broomfield as 'star'

Nick Broomfield is probably one of the few British documentary-makers that students will have heard of and may well recognise. His early style was observational (*Juvenile Liaison*, 1975 and *Tattooed Tears*, 1978), influenced by the direct cinema documentary-maker Fred Wiseman and made in collaboration with Joan Churchill. His films from the mid-1980s onwards have shifted in style from the observational, where the director does not appear, to the performative, where Nick Broomfield has the starring role. For more information on Broomfield's biography and films including extracts and interviews, see www.screenonline/documentary.

Star studies

In film theory, the study of stars is usually based on fiction films where there is an acceptance that there is a difference between the person off screen, the actor, and the roles that they play on screen – although there is often perceived to be an overlap between the two. The relatively few actors who become stars in Hollywood have developed a persona – a particular character that the audience expects to see each time they appear. The persona is made up from a mixture of the films the star appears in and what is known – or suggested – about their private lives. In documentary the link between the persona – the on-screen performance – and the real person seems much closer. We expect Michael Moore to be the same in real life as he is on screen – but of course his on-screen appearances may well be his performance of a documentary-maker.

Discussion point

'Real people' who appear in documentaries have been referred to as social actors, emphasising the way that being filmed can alter a person's behaviour.

- Is it possible for subjects of documentary to behave the same on camera as off?
- What effect does the concept of social actors have on definitions of documentary realism?

Defining the star persona

In developing a persona, a star may retain continuity throughout their roles with their use of:

- Voice
- Gesture
- Movement
- Costume style
- Attitude.

These elements combine to create a persona which carries with it meanings and connotations, often to do with gender, sexuality and national identity. To analyse this meaning, Thompson (1978) developed the commutation test. Originally applied to fiction films, it can also be used with documentary. The test relies on Saussure's theory that a sign is made up of two parts – the signifier and the signified – that are culturally specific. Therefore in reference to film stars, while an image (the signifier) may denote a film star – Brad Pitt – the image will also connote further meanings such as masculinity, attractiveness, Americanness. In turn this might suggest that stars are not chosen by an audience and promoted by the industry by chance but because they embody ideological meanings. The premise of the commutation test is that it foregrounds the constructed nature of the persona by exchanging one star for another in the same role, eg replace Tom Cruise with Tom Hanks in any of his roles to understand their different signifiers.

Nick Broomfield's persona

In his performative documentaries, it is possible to recognise certain characteristics constituting the Nick Broomfield persona that can be analysed with reference to the above definitions.

- Voice. Broomfield's voice is a distinctive feature of the documentaries as it is heard in voiceover and in on-screen questions. It is recognisably English upper middle class, relatively high-pitched but with a drawl which creates a sardonic effect. In the context of Broomfield's American-set documentaries, his identifiable Englishness is important as it feeds into the interviewee's preconceptions about him.
- Costume style. Typical attire is either a leather or green 'bomber' jacket, a white T-shirt or shirt and jeans. These are obviously practical clothes but the army connotation of the jacket encourages the perception, often created in the films, of Broomfield battling against authority (the leather jacket has similar anti-authority connotations). The costume also creates a tougher edge to the character than other aspects of the persona might suggest. This tough edge is reinforced by the short and spiky haircut. The most iconic aspects of Broomfield's image are the props he wears and carries: the large headphones and microphone boom, a constant reminder – to the audience and the interviewees – that he is a documentary-maker, not just a presenter. (The recognition of Broomfield's persona was evident in the TV adverts for Volkswagen in the 1990s.) The reinforcement of his professional status is often in contrast to his seemingly bumbling, self-deprecating manner.
- Broomfield's technique in interviewing is to ask very few questions. This has the effect of making the interviewee keep talking, perhaps saying things that they might regret. It can also have the effect of making the interviewee frustrated and angry (this is particularly revealing in the interviews with Courtney Love's father in *Kurt and Courtney*). His questions are often put with a puzzled air as if he can't quite understand what the subject means, a strategy that also encourages the interviewee to be less guarded.

Overall, these characteristics create a persona based on a series of contradictions around appearing amateur and professional and this is crucial in encouraging relationships with his subjects. Broomfield himself has referred to this persona, asked '[why] he appears a little stupid on screen' when 'he seems intelligent in real life', he responded that his 'smiley persona has proved most useful in getting his subjects to open up on camera' (Bruzzi, 2000). In Jon Ronson (2002), 'The Egos Have Landed', Ronson, also a performative documentary-maker, refers to the persona created by Broomfield (and Moore, Theroux and himself) as 'faux naïf'.

Discussion point

What similarities and differences are there between the personas of Nick Broomfield and Michael Moore? Consider costume, voice, interview techniques. Why do you think it tends to be men who make this kind of documentary? Do the personas tell us anything about our expectations of gender? Would a female interviewer with a similar persona get a different response?

Teaching tip

The commutation test can be used in analysing the persona constructed by the documentary-maker. Once students have listed the characteristic elements of, for example, Nick Broomfield, they can 'replace' him with another persona (not necessarily another documentary-maker). Once they have chosen, ask students to pick a scene from the documentary and analyse how a change in persona could alter the meaning of that particular scene and of the documentary as a whole.

Authorship theory

Certain documentary-makers can be considered auteurs in the same way that directors of fiction films are. To be defined as an auteur, a filmmaker (usually the director) must have a body of work that reveals a consistency of film style and themes. This is often defined as a recognisable signature that makes it possible to identify a film as being by a specific director (eg Ford, Hitchcock, Scorsese) and also reveals the worldview of that director. Since its development in France in the 1950s, authorship theory has been increasingly criticised for its traditional view of cinema. Authorship emphasises the idea that a film is the creation of an individual – this was challenged by developments in genre theory and authorship studies.

Auteur structuralism

In the 1970s a new development in film theory accepted the concept of authorship in cinema but questioned how the theory might be used. Auteur structuralism (Wollen, 1972) argued that the auteur identified within the film – the artist with a particular worldview, ideology etc – only exists within the film itself and not outside it. It was therefore pointless to try and trace the style and meaning of a film back to the director's experience and biography. In auteur structuralism the term auteur is used to signify the way in which a range of narrative, thematic and stylistic structures can be identified across a group of films. These films can then be referred to as 'Scorsese' films or 'Tarantino' films as a way of categorising and understanding cinema – but not to state that the films reveal anything about the director beyond the film. In other words, the director 'Scorsese' identifiable in *Taxi Driver* (Martin Scorsese, US, 1976), *Raging Bull* (Martin Scorsese, US, 1980) etc is different from Scorsese the real person.

Bruzzi (2000) applies this approach to Broomfield as an auteur and star. As a star, Nick Broomfield appears as 'Nick Broomfield' the self-deprecating, slightly bumbling filmmaker, which is different from Nick Broomfield the real person. This is also true of Nick Broomfield the director. There is a difference between the director who appears on screen ('Nick Broomfield') and the auteur putting together the finished film that we are watching. Finally, there is a difference between the 'documentary' we watch being made in front of us (full of setbacks, mistakes, seemingly improvised) and the finished, carefully constructed film.

This analysis of 'Nick Broomfield' is useful in understanding the constructed nature of all documentary but particularly the performative mode and analysing the effect of these constructions on the audience.

Worksheet 18 Performative documentary conventions

Students are asked to identify and analyse the use of film language in the two documentaries. In addition to developing their knowledge of documentary techniques this worksheet also forms the basis for later work on Broomfield as an auteur.

Film extracts: Opening of *Kurt and Courtney* (first five minutes) and opening of *Aileen* (first six minutes)

To access student worksheets and other online materials go to *Teaching Film and TV Documentary* at **www.bfi.org.uk/tfms** and enter User name: **docs@bfi.org.uk** and Password: **te1612do**.

worksheet 18 **Performative documentary conventions**

This worksheet asks you to identify and analyse the use of film language in the two performative documentaries you are studying. This analysis will form the basis of a definition of performative documentary.

Resources: Film extracts for analysis:
- Opening of *Kurt and Courtney* (Nick Broomfield, UK, 1998) (first five minutes);
- Opening of *Aileen: Life and Death of a Serial Killer* (Nick Broomfield, UK, 2003) (first six minutes).

Activity 1

After watching each extract make notes on the following, giving an example from the film:

- Which types of footage are used in the opening? Why do you think the different types have been used – what is their function?
- What documentary techniques can you identify in the sequence?
- What information is given by the voiceover? What is the relationship between the voiceover and the images?
- What do we find out about the central subject?
- How is the opening sequence of a documentary similar to the opening sequence of a fiction film (eg introduction of characters, situation, plot, themes, attempt to attract and keep audience attention)?

Aileen

Page 1 of 1   Film and TV Documentary

1 of 2 pages

Both extracts set up the background to the story (exposition), introduce the main characters, themes and the visual style.

Points to note

- Both openings use a range of archive material: news footage, home movies, stills, press conferences and in *Aileen* extracts from Broomfield's earlier documentary, to provide exposition for the audience.
- They both start with a voiceover by Broomfield relating a violent death. Information about the incident is given in a factual way, with reference to police reports.
- The voiceover becomes increasingly subjective so that the filmmaker's position becomes clear to the audience.
- Both films are structured around a journey and an investigation, elements emphasised by the use of point-of-view shots from the car travelling along the road.
- References to the filmmaking process – problems with financing and the negative influence of Courtney Love in *Kurt and Courtney*, the corrupt police in *Aileen*.

Worksheet 19 Performative documentary and audience manipulation

Students are asked to construct an analysis of the way that sympathy and identification with particular characters is created in the documentaries and to discuss the effect of this on the audience. This worksheet is applied to the whole of each film – rather than extracts – although students could choose an area to concentrate on as representative once they've considered the film as a whole.

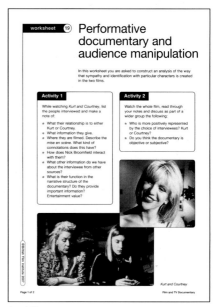

worksheet 19 **Performative documentary and audience manipulation**

In this worksheet you are asked to construct an analysis of the way that sympathy and identification with particular characters is created in the two films.

Activity 1

While watching *Kurt and Courtney*, list the people interviewed and make a note of:

- What their relationship is to either Kurt or Courtney.
- What information they give.
- Where they are filmed. Describe the mise en scène. What kind of connotations does this have?
- How does Nick Broomfield interact with them?
- What other information do we have about the interviewee from other sources?
- What is their function in the narrative structure of the documentary? Do they provide important information? Entertainment value?

Activity 2

Watch the whole film, read through your notes and discuss as part of a wider group the following:

- Who is more positively represented by the choice of interviewees? Kurt or Courtney?
- Do you think the documentary is objective or subjective?

Kurt and Courtney

Page 1 of 2   Film and TV Documentary

1 of 2 pages

In *Kurt and Courtney*, the aim of the filmmaker is to get the audience to take sides – with Kurt Cobain (or his supporters) and against Courtney Love. This is done through the construction of very different representations of the two main characters.

Points to note

- The interviewees who are sympathetic to Kurt are interviewed in their own familiar surroundings and are treated sensitively. The *mise en scène* is important – Kurt Cobain's aunt is interviewed next to religious imagery; his ex-schoolteacher sits in a classroom surrounded by books – and creates an image of respectability and trustworthiness which reflects Kurt Cobain's life pre-Courtney Love.
- The type of people interviewed changes as the documentary develops, moving from the mainstream to people on the edges of society, from light and open rooms to dark and claustrophobic basements. This mirrors the changes in Kurt's life with the – bad – influence of Courtney Love.
- The information given by interviewees about Kurt creates the impression of an innocent who was corrupted, someone who was spiritual and not interested in material wealth until he met Love.
- No interviewees speak positively about Courtney Love – even her father accuses her of murder.
- Footage of Courtney on a chat show and at the Oscars ceremony emphasises the superficiality of her life in contrast to the more authentic people who loved Kurt.
- Neither Kurt nor Courtney can be interviewed for the documentary, which means that the images created can never be challenged directly. (In documentary the people who aren't interviewed can be as important in creating a particular argument as those who are.)
- When faced with evidence that Kurt Cobain was not as innocent as the image created in the documentary suggests, eg the answerphone recording of him threatening a journalist, Nick Broomfield assumes that this is a result of Courtney Love's influence.
- The completion of the documentary is threatened by Courtney. She will not allow Nirvana's music to be used on the soundtrack and apparently put pressure on some of the financial backers to withdraw money from the project, but no explanation is given for these actions.
- As part of the narrative structure of the documentary, it is helpful to have a series of obstacles for the filmmaker to overcome and these are provided by Courtney Love. The ongoing suggestion that she is dangerous and has powerful friends also means that Nick Broomfield is presented in a more heroic light.

In *Aileen*, there is a similar form of audience manipulation, in this case aimed at creating some understanding of why Aileen Wournos committed the crimes she did. It is also part of a wider argument that exposes the inequalities of the US legal system and is against the death penalty.

While the documentary never attempts to justify or excuse Aileen's crimes, she is represented as a vulnerable person who has been abused throughout her life and has now fallen victim to a legal system which privileges the wealthy.

Points to note

- The appeal hearing at the beginning of the film allows the audience to hear about Aileen's abusive childhood.
- Aileen's mother left home when she was a child and she was raised by her grandfather, who is believed to be the father of her child.
- Aileen was forced to live in the woods near her home as a teenager.
- Some of the police involved in her case were suspended for selling their stories to the press and attempting to make deals in Hollywood.
- Aileen is represented as protective of her girlfriend (who also betrays her).
- We are shown some skilful and creative drawings done by Aileen and kept by her friend that suggest another side to her character.
- The lawyer who defended Aileen at her murder trial, Dr Legal, is shown to be incompetent.
- The documentary suggests that Aileen is executed for political reasons (it's an election year) despite the fact that she is probably mentally ill.
- It is clear from his voiceover ('I felt so much sympathy for Aileen') and anger at her execution that Nick Broomfield feels that Aileen has been treated terribly – whatever her crimes – and this is likely to affect the audience reaction.

Teaching tip

In the appeal hearing at the beginning of the film, Nick Broomfield is subpoenaed and questioned about his documentary techniques. He is accused by the prosecution lawyer of 'cutting and pasting' to create a particular affect in *Aileen Wournos: The Selling of a Serial Killer*. This is a useful scene to discuss with students as it illustrates the constructed nature of documentary and also the common misapprehension that documentary is a direct representation of reality (the prosecutor refers to editing as if it were the same as lying). These ideas could be developed by considering other examples where a documentary has been used as evidence in court – eg the Michael Jackson trial where Martin Bashir was called to give evidence in a similar way regarding his documentary about Jackson.

Worksheet 20 Nick Broomfield as auteur

This worksheet builds on the previous areas of study into the two films. It asks students to analyse the way that Nick Broomfield can be defined as an auteur in terms of documentary style and themes.

To access student worksheets and other online materials go to *Teaching Film and TV Documentary* at **www.bfi.org.uk/tfms** and enter User name: **docs@bfi.org.uk** and Password: **te1612do**.

In order to complete the worksheet, students need to have an understanding of what an auteur is. The following textbooks have sections on authorship: *The Media Student's Book* (Branston and Stafford, 1998), *An Introduction to Film Studies* (Nelmes, 1996), *Teach Yourself Film Studies* (Buckland, 1998). Also see *Teaching Auteur Study* by David Wharton and Jeremy Grant (2005).

Drawing on the idea of auteur structuralism, it also addresses the relative contribution of auteur and the pre-existing form. This is an activity that draws on the complete films but also offers two sequences illustrating the Broomfield signature for analysis.

Points to note

- Both films use the conventions of the performative mode (as previously outlined).
- The voiceover is subjective, recording the filmmaker's reaction to events.
- The filmmaker appears on screen and has a recognisable persona.
- Both films follow an investigative narrative structure, the focus of which is likely to change as the documentary progresses:

1. *Kurt and Courtney* begins as an investigation into the conspiracy theories around Kurt Cobain's death; then transforms into the question of whether Courtney Love had him killed; then culminates as an attempt to interview Love and investigate her personality.
2. In *Aileen*, Broomfield is forced into the story as a witness; then endeavours to discover why Aileen committed her crimes; before progressing into a campaign to have her death sentence reprieved.

- The overall style of the films is immediate and improvised; everything seems to happen in the present with minimal planning – this is emphasised by the shifting focus as well as the 'mistakes' that are left in the film. In *Kurt and Courtney*, Broomfield walks into the wrong apartment when going to interview one of Kurt's friends. This is a way of reassuring the audience of the realism of what they are seeing.
- Both films deal with American society and specifically what happens to people who are disenfranchised. This is apparent in both the content but also the form of the documentaries where the focus moves from the apparent centre of the film to the supporting characters.
- The supporting characters tend to be unusual, damaged or quirky which also adds interest and entertainment value to the documentary. Il Duce in *Kurt and Courtney* is a particularly memorable character.
- Both films have themes about fame and celebrity in the US, questioning both the nature of fame and also its effects on the famous. In both cases, celebrity is seen as corrupting and dangerous.

Nick Broomfield can be defined as an auteur in terms of the consistency of style and themes across his work but it could also be argued that this is as much to do with working within a particular genre – the performative documentary – as with an individual signature. It is also worth noting that Joan Churchill has a co-directing and cinematography credit on the film.

Film extracts

The final sequences in *Kurt and Courtney* (final six minutes from the ACLU awards ceremony) and *Aileen* (final six minutes, from the end of Aileen's press conference).

Both these final sequences highlight a main area of controversy in the performative mode as Nick Broomfield becomes part of the action rather than merely observing and recording events. The sequences are good examples of the way in which the interaction between the filmmaker and subject can become the focus of the film as well as illustrating the 'Nick Broomfield' persona. There is no attempt at objectivity in these moments and it could be argued that this is a more truthful representation of events. It is also clear that the definition of a documentary as a record of events which would take place whether or not the documentary-maker is there recording them no longer applies.

The final extracts share a similar structure that could also be seen as typical of Broomfield's work. Both involve:

- A final 'interview' with the subject of the film.
- A Nick Broomfield speech clarifying his point of view.
- Calm and poignant final shots, with a piece of music relevant to the subject.

● Criticisms of the performative mode

This mode of documentary is controversial because:

- It breaks down the boundaries between the observer and the observed.
- The documentary-maker alters the course of events and/or makes things happen.
- The close relationship that develops between the interviewees and filmmaker can affect behaviour on screen – and leave people vulnerable once filming is finished.

This criticism is summed up by Andrew Jarecki (*Capturing the Friedmans*, US, 2003):

> 90 per cent of the time when I see that [the documentary-maker on camera] I find it intrusive and unnecessary, because unless you genuinely are the central character, it can be a relatively lazy way of making a film: you can end up being a walking apologist for what's missing. (Sweet, 2004)

Discussion point

What is more truthful in documentary – for the process of documentary-making to be made visible or to be kept hidden? If a documentary is always going to be subjective, is it more honest to make that subjectivity clear?

Suggestions for further work

Kurt and Courtney could be used as part of a study of documentaries about music and the music industry that could also include:

Biggie and Tupac (Nick Broomfield, UK, 2002)
Gimme Shelter (Albert and David Maysles, US, 1970)
Don't Look Back (D A Pennebaker, US, 1967)
Geri (Molly Dineen, UK, 2001)
In Bed with Madonna (Alek Keshishian, US, 1991)
Awesome: I Fuckin' Shot That! (Adam Yauch, US, 2006)
New York Doll (Greg Whiteley, US, 2005)
Glastonbury (Julien Temple, UK, 2006)
Bloc Party (Michel Gondry, US, 2006)

● The drama-documentary

A different way of approaching documentary as performance is through the use of dramatic enactments, which can range from short reconstructions of events within a documentary to the use of professional actors and narrative techniques from fiction films. The melding of factual and fictional forms in documentary is one that has become increasingly controversial but also popular with institutions and audiences.

> Depending on which interpreters are read, the meeting of fact and fiction results in either the subversion of documentary claims to authenticity and veracity, or, innovative and productive approaches to documentary representation. (Beattie, 2004)

Defining drama-documentary

This is a difficult form to place in specific categories and conventions because:

- The terms drama-documentary and docudrama are often used interchangeably.
- There are related forms such as docusoap and faction.
- Definitions rely on the premise that there are oppositions of definition, where documentary = fact and drama = fiction, when the two forms have always merged.

Historical context

The formal mix of factual events and fictional techniques has a long history – although the term drama-documentary did not become common until the 1960s. Some early films using this approach include:

The Birth of a Nation (D W Griffith, US, 1915)
Controversial history of the Civil War told from the perspective of the South.
Battleship Potemkin (Sergei Eisenstein, USSR, 1925)
Celebration of the mutiny on the Potemkin in 1905 includes the Odessa Steps sequence where the Tsarist Cossacks attack the mutineers. Although this event has become a symbol of the Russian Revolution, it was probably invented.
Nanook of the North (Robert Flaherty, US/France, 1922)
Influential documentary containing many (uncredited) reconstructions of Inuit life, including practices that were already archaic.
Fires Were Started (Humphrey Jennings, UK, 1943)
Part of a series of films made for the Ministry of Information, *Fires Were Started* used a script as well as a mix of professional and non-professional actors to follow the work of the fire brigade during the Blitz.

One of the reasons for the development of this hybrid form can be seen in the fact that all these films are examples of propaganda. The controversy surrounding drama-documentary is usually to do with its ideological purpose and this may be one of the reasons that the form developed – it is a very successful persuasive form. The criticism of drama-documentary as ideological again raises the issue that most people perceive more 'traditional' documentary as being factual and objective.

Other reasons for the development of drama-documentary are:

- Lack of access to subject. The contemporary drama-documentary was developed as part of the *World in Action* current affairs series (Granada, 1963–98) in the 1960s. One of the most important stories at the time was the Cold War but the programme-makers had no access to the USSR and so increasingly turned to dramatic reconstructions and then to drama-documentary.
- Representation of historical events. The mix of drama and documentary techniques provided a new perspective on the past; 'bringing it to life' for the audience but also presenting a specific point of view. The most influential example of this approach was *Culloden* (BBC, 1964).
- Danger to interviewees/witnesses. The drama-documentary enabled the statements of people who needed to remain anonymous to be heard without endangering them.
- Entertaining the audience. The drama-documentary developed on television and can be seen as part of the need to create new forms to attract audiences who had perhaps become bored by more straightforward factual programming.

In studying the drama-documentary, it is helpful to begin by thinking about degrees of fictionalisation ranging from re-enactment with actors and scripts to the use of trial, inquest or enquiry transcripts as the basis for the text. This last approach has become increasingly used in theatre: *The Colour of Justice*, based on the Macpherson Report on the investigation into Stephen Lawrence's death and *Justifying War*, based on the Hutton Report into the decision to go to war in Iraq.

Teaching tip

There is such a range of television programmes and feature films based on 'real events' that definitions can become meaningless and anything with reference to some actual event is defined as drama-documentary. To develop a more useful categorisation, ask students to think where their chosen examples would fit on a spectrum with fact at one end and fiction at the other. They would need to justify the placement with reference to techniques used, real events, people, places, transcripts, public statements, private conversations and actors.

Key films

Festival (Annie Griffin, UK, 2005)
Bloody Sunday (Paul Greengrass, UK, 2002)

Festival

Festival follows the experiences of a group of different performers, their managers and journalists during the Edinburgh Festival.

Factual techniques:

- The film was shot during the festival and includes footage of performers, audience members and tourists.
- The film uses the visual language of observational documentary-making: hand-held, mobile camerawork which follows the subjects, natural lighting and real locations.
- The journalist, Joan Gerard, works for BBC Scotland and conducts vox pops with real people in the street about their reactions to the Festival.
- The Edinburgh Fringe Festival is an actual event.

Fictional techniques:

- *Festival* was written and directed by Annie Griffin who also wrote *The Book Group* (Channel 4, 2002–3).
- The multistrand narrative cuts between a variety of characters – about 13 – commenting on the experiences and personalities of unrelated characters.
- The different narrative strands build towards a conclusion and in some cases resolution.
- The film features professional actors – some fairly well known from film and television (Daniela Nardini is the journalist).

Some aspects of the film don't fit neatly into either category:

- Central to the narrative is a comedy award that is obviously based on the Perrier Award, although it is given a different name.
- There has been speculation that some of the characters, particularly the comics, are based on real people.
- Some of the scenes were improvised.

Despite these grey areas, it should be possible for students to decide to what extent this is a drama or a documentary and how the different forms are mixed. This becomes clearer with the use of contrasting examples:

Bloody Sunday

Bloody Sunday follows the events of January 30, 1972, in Derry, when 13 people were shot dead by the British Army while taking part in a civil rights protest against internment.

Factual techniques:

- The film is based on the real events of Bloody Sunday, January 1972 as told by a range of different people involved. Many of the accounts come from the book *Eyewitness, Bloody Sunday* by Don Mullan.
- Some of the dialogue is in the form of public record, such as press conferences.
- The central character, Ivan Cooper MP, is a real person.
- The names and number of those who died are verifiable and the coroner's transcripts are used.
- *Bloody Sunday* is filmed using documentary techniques.

Fictional techniques:

- The real events are organised into a narrative structure, moving from dawn to dusk and begins and ends with Ivan Cooper giving a press conference. This mirroring technique suggests a symmetry not usually evident in real life.
- While Ivan Cooper is a real person, other characters are composites or created to represent a particular point of view.
- Dialogue is used to create character rather than as an accurate record of what was said.

Bloody Sunday was an extremely controversial film, with critics questioning the legitimacy of using the drama-documentary for such a difficult and contentious subject. Central to the controversy was that in *Bloody Sunday* the British army is shown as firing the first bullet into the marchers, rather than being provoked and retaliating – something which had been the centre of political and judicial debate. It is these decisions that mark out drama-documentary as an ideological form.

Drama-documentary and documentary drama (docudrama)

In designating a range of texts along a fiction and fact spectrum one of the clearest distinctions can be between drama-documentary and documentary drama. This distinction relies on whether the events depicted are real or made up and the 'look' of the text. Caughie (1981) argues that drama-documentary is based on investigation and research of real events but uses the conventions of fictional forms to tell the story. Documentary drama in contrast uses the documentary visual style to tell an invented, although possible, story. It is evident that since this distinction was made, there has been a further blurring in terms of look and visual style, but the central premise of fictional and non-fictional events is often still clear.

Key examples of drama-documentary

Who Bombed Birmingham? (ITV, 1990)
Death of a Princess (Granada, 1980)
The Queen's Sister (Simon Cellan Jones, UK, 2005)
The Deal (Stephen Frears, UK, 2004)
The Queen (Stephen Frears, UK/France/Italy, 2006)
The Hamburg Cell (Channel 4, 2004)
Shipman (ITV, 2002)
The Government Inspector (Channel 4, 2005)
United 93 (Paul Greengrass, US/UK/France, 2006)

Key examples of docudrama

Cathy Come Home (Ken Loach, UK, 1966)
Scum (Alan Clarke, UK, 1977)
Days of Hope (BBC, 1975)
Ghostwatch (BBC1, 1992)
Out of Control (BBC1, 2002)
Supervolcano (BBC1, 2005)

What if?

A further complication in defining this form is a related mode that has become known as 'What if?' or the mock documentary (or even, mockumentary), which uses documentary techniques to speculate about past or future events.

These include:

- *It Happened Here* (Kevin Brownlow and Andrew Rollo, UK, 1966), which imagines what would have happened if the Nazis had invaded Britain.
- *The War Game* (Peter Watkins, 1965) where the speculation is based on the effect of a nuclear attack (and was banned by the BBC which had originally commissioned it).
- *Punishment Park* (Peter Watkins, UK, 1971), set in Vietnam-era America where criticism of the state has been outlawed.
- *CSA: Confederate States of America* (Kevin Wilmot, US, 2005), a supposedly 'BBC'-produced documentary, which asks what life would be like if the South had won the Civil War and slavery had been made legal.
- A series of recent BBC films: *Smallpox* (BBC, 2002) (see the BBC website for a useful article on the making of 'What if?'-style documentary drama at: www.bbc.co.uk/drama/smallpox2002) and *The Day Britain Stopped*, (BBC, 2003). Some of the issues arising from using this approach are discussed at: www.news.bbc.co.uk/1/hi/the_day_britain_stopped.

Paul Greengrass and drama-documentary

Paul Greengrass has become one of the key figures in the development of this genre, working for *World in Action* (Granada) and then making *The Murder of Stephen Lawrence* (1999) which covered the murder, the police investigation and inquiry. *Bloody Sunday* was heavily influenced by *The Battle of Algiers* (Gillo Pontecorvo, Algeria/Italy, 1966) another drama-documentary about an occupying power and its brutality (the French in Algeria). Greengrass's work is interesting because of the way it defies easy categorisation in terms of fact, fiction, drama and documentary:

> What I wanted to do was make a film that tapped into what I think is going on out there, which is doubt, mistrust and questioning .... It is quite clear that the Government hasn't been telling us the truth about the most important issues of all, like why we went to war. It is quite clear that the secret parts of the Government let us down profoundly.
> Interview with Paul Greengrass (12/09/06, www.timesonline.co.uk)

Greengrass was not talking about drama-documentary here but discussing his Hollywood film, *The Bourne Supremacy* (US, 2004) which, with its semi-documentary style and subject matter apparently based on real (if exaggerated) political events, provides food for further discussion.

United 93 *(Paul Greengrass, US/UK/France, 2006)*

The recent release of *United 93* has been particularly controversial and illustrates some concerns and criticisms surrounding the drama-documentary form:

- Trailers for the film were withdrawn from New York cinemas because people claimed that it was 'too soon' for such an event to be turned into a film.
- Its attempt to make the audience feel part of events in the cabin of the plane led to the film being accused of voyeurism.
- Because no one on board survived, many of the conversations between characters are scripted but, according to critics, the audience often accepts them as real.
- Critics argue that there was no need to make this film; unlike the more investigative drama-documentaries, it does not reveal conspiracy or corruption.

Teaching tip

Ask students to debate the ethical dilemmas of the docudrama by discussing:

- Intended aim and function
- Concept of voyeurism
- Relationship between documentary and truth.

To give the discussion focus, students could begin by reading two pieces (a review and a feature) on *United 93:* Ali Jafaar, 'Review of United 93', available at: www.bfi.org.uk/sightandsound/review/3315 and David Osbourne, 'Cinema Tackles Terror: Courage on a Day of Death', available at: www.enjoyment.independent.co.uk/film/features/article360402.

For each review, ask students to note whether or not the writer thinks the film should have been made, giving evidence from the article for each point. This can then form the basis of a discussion.

To develop these ideas further, students could research the response to Oliver Stone's *World Trade Center* (US, 2006), a fictional account of the experience of two firemen on 9/11.

Suggestions for further work

Alternative approaches for studying the work of Paul Greengrass:

- An auteur study. The themes of injustices suffered by ordinary people and the corruption of state institutions explored within a consistent visual style.
- A British film director. Greengrass can be seen as part of the tradition of British social realism, influenced by directors such as Alan Clarke and Ken Loach.

Worksheet 21 Developing a drama-documentary

As a way of reviewing the different areas of the drama-documentary studied, this worksheet is a simulation exercise. Students are asked to consider the different processes and pressures involved in making drama-documentary.

To access student worksheets and other online materials go to *Teaching Film and TV Documentary* at **www.bfi.org.uk/tfms** and enter User name: **docs@bfi.org.uk** and Password: **te1612do**.

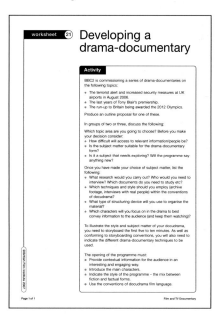

Glossary

Auteur/author

A film director with consistent themes and a style which is identifiable across a body of work.

Convergence

The way global media technology companies break down the barriers between IT, media and communications technology. An example of this is that one format can be accessed by television, mobile and online all owned by the same corporation.

Direct cinema

A type of observational documentary filmmaking, the direct cinema movement was developed in the US in the 1960s by the Maysles brothers, D A Pennebaker and Robert Drew. The aim of direct cinema is to record life as it is lived and is often described as 'fly-on-the-wall' filmmaking.

Docudrama

A hybrid form which uses the documentary visual style to tell an invented – although possible – story.

Documentary realism

A film aesthetic that signifies the real world through the use of location shooting, voiceover, interviews etc.

Docusoap

Television format which follows 'ordinary people' who are linked by a particular job or institution and uses soap opera conventions – melodrama, cliff hangers etc – to shape the narrative.

Drama-documentary

Hybrid form based on the investigation into real events which uses the conventions of fictional forms – script, actors, narrative structure etc – to tell the story.

Exposition

Explanatory sequence in fiction and non-fiction films which provides important contextual information for the audience; this may be done through dialogue, sound or images.

Fly-on-the-wall

A style of documentary attempting to represent events with minimal intervention. This relies on the development of lightweight mobile camera, sound and lighting technology and attempts to make the audience feel as if they are present at the situation being filmed. This is a convention of the observational mode of documentary-making.

Free cinema

A British documentary film movement of the 1950s which used a mixture of observational and poetic techniques to represent working class subject matter. Several of the directors associated with the movement became part of the British new wave – Lindsay Anderson, Tony Richardson and Karel Reisz.

Ideology

Dominant ideology is a system of ideas, values and beliefs promoted by dominant groups (institutions of state, corporations etc) to reinforce their power.

Mass observation

A social research study set up in 1937 to create a record of everyday life in Britain. Some 500 volunteers kept diaries of their experiences and these formed the basis of academic study. Mass observation was closed in the 1950s but restarted in 1981.

Mise en scène

The visual elements of a film (in fiction film assumed to be under the control of the director) which create meaning for the audience.

Mode of address

The way in which any media text chooses to address its audience and how the audience (subject of the text), is positioned by that mode of address. This can be read through analysis of signs and reveals the assumptions that the producer has about the audience as well as defining the target audience.

Modernism

The general term for a range of European artistic and cultural movements which emerged in the beginning of the twentieth century. Modernist artists developed revolutionary styles in opposition to more traditional forms in art, literature and architecture. Modernism is particularly associated with forms of abstract rather than figurative art.

Polemic

A strongly expressed, passionate argument, usually on a controversial subject; a polemic is explicitly subjective, taking a position for or against someone or something.

Propaganda

The systematic dissemination – via a range of art and media including film – of deceptive or distorted information which relies on an emotional appeal to provoke a response.

Realism

An aesthetic found in a range of art forms which aims to show the world as it is, with the emphasis often on socially marginalized groups.

Representation

The way in which particular groups etc are represented in media texts, which can be analysed to assess social effects.

Social actors

The term used to describe the role of 'real people' in a documentary. The use of the term suggests that everyone who appears in a documentary behaves differently from how they would off screen.

Surrealism

Art movement of the 1920s, whose followers believed in the superiority of the unconscious mind over the material world. Key figures such as Breton, Buñuel and Dali explored ways of representing the workings of the mind in literature, film and painting, developing a style that juxtaposed unexpected and inexplicable images.

Voyeurism

Used in the context of the ethical debates around documentary-making, particularly the observational and reality modes, voyeurism refers to the pleasure of secret observation and is often associated with sexual or sordid subject matter.

References and resources

Bibliography

I Aitken (1997), 'The British Documentary Movement', in R Murphy (ed), *The British Cinema Book*, BFI

E Barnouw (1993), *Documentary*, OUP

A Bazin, H Gray (1960) 'The Ontology of the Photographic Image', Film Quarterly, (Vol 13, No 4 Summer, pp4-9)

K Beattie (2004), *Documentary Screens: Nonfiction Film and Television*, Palgrave Macmillan

D Bordwell and K Thompson (1993), *Film Art*, McGraw Hill

J Butler (1993), 'Gender is Burning: Questions of Appropriation and Subversion', in Thornham, S (Ed) (1999) *Feminist Film Theory, a Reader*, Edinburgh University Press

G Branston and R Stafford (1998), *The Media Student's Book*, Routledge

T de Bromhead (1996), *Looking Two Ways*, Intervention Press

S Bruzzi (2000), *New Documentary: A Critical Introduction*, Routledge

W Buckland (1998), *Teach Yourself Film Studies*, Hodder and Stoughton

J Caughie (1981), 'Progressive Television and Documentary Drama', in T Bennett *et al* (eds), *Popular Television and Film*, BFI

J Corner (2000), 'What Can We Say about Documentary?', *Media, Culture and Society* 22:5

J Corner (2001), 'Documentary Realism', in G Creeber (ed), *The Television Genre Book*, BFI

D De Nitto (1985), *Film, Form and Feeling*, Harper and Row

C Flinn (1998), 'Containing Fire: Performance in Paris is Burning' in *Documenting the Documentary*, ed Barry Keith Grant and Jeannette Sloniowski (Wayne State University Press)

N Higham (2001), 'The End of Reality TV', 22 May, BBC News Online

B Holm and G Quimby (1980), *Edward S. Curtis in the Land of the War Canoes*, University of Washington Press

J Izod and R Kilborn (1998), 'The Documentary', in J Hill and P Church Gibson (eds), *The Oxford Guide to Film Studies*, Oxford University Press

J Izod and R Kilborn (1997), *An Introduction to Television Documentary: Confronting Reality*, Manchester University Press

J Izod *et al* (2000), *From Grierson to the Docusoap: Breaking the Boundaries*, University of Luton Press

S Koch (1991), *Stargazer*, Marion Boyars

K MacDonald and M Cousins (eds) (1996), *Imagining Reality: The Faber Book of Documentary*, Faber and Faber

J Nelmes (1996), *An Introduction to Film Studies*, Routledge

B Nichols (1991), *Representing Reality*, Indiana University Press

B Nichols (1994), *Blurred Boundaries*, Indiana University Press

B Nichols (2001), *Introduction to Documentary*, Indiana University Press

D Paget (1990), *True Stories*, Manchester University Press

J Ronson (2002), 'The Egos Have Landed', *Sight and Sound*, November, BFI

P Rotha (1973), *Documentary Diary*, Secker and Warburg

M Sweet (2004), 'Point and Shoot', 23 May, *The Independent on Sunday*

M Sweney (2006), 'The Big internet Streaming Question', *Media Guardian*, 11 July

J Thompson (1978) 'Screen Acting and the Commutation Test', *Screen* (Vol 19, no 2, Summer, pp55-69)

C Tryhorn (2005), 'Ofcom Confirms Old Media Fears', *Media Guardian*, 10 August

P Wells (2000), 'The Documentary', in J Nelmes, *An Introduction to Film Studies*, Routledge

B Winston (1995), *Claiming the Real: The Documentary Film Revisited,* BFI

B Winston (1999), 'The Primrose Path: Faking UK Television Documentary, Docuglitz and Docusoap', *Screening the Past*, available at: www.latrobe.edu.au/screeningthepast/firstrelease/fr1199/bwfr8b.htm

P Wollen (1972), *Signs and Meanings*, Secker and Warburg

J Wood (2005), *Nick Broomfield*: *Documenting Icons*, Faber and Faber

Filmography

A detailed **filmography** is available at www.bfi.org.uk/tfms. Go to the page for *Teaching Film and TV Documentary*, and enter username: **docs@bfi.org.uk** Password: **te1612do**

7 UP (Granada, 1964)
999 (BBC1, 1993–2001)
Aileen Wuornos: The Selling of a Serial Killer (Nick Broomfield, UK, 1992)
Aileen: Life and Death of a Serial Killer (Nick Broomfield, UK, 2003)

Airline (ITV, 1999)

Airport (BBC, 1997)

Albert Maysles: The Poetic Eye (BBC4, 2006)

Animal Hospital (BBC1, 1985–2004)

Apprentice, The (BBC2, 2005)

Arrival of a Train (Louis Lumière, France, 1895)

Awesome: I Fuckin' Shot That! (Adam Yauch, US, 2006)

Battle of Algiers, The (Gillo Pontecorvo, Algeria/Italy, 1966)

Battleship Potemkin (Sergei Eisenstein, USSR, 1925)

Big Brother (Channel 4 and E4, 2000–present)

Biggie and Tupac (Nick Broomfield, UK, 2002)

Bill, The (ITV, 1994–present)

Birth of a Nation, The (D W Griffith, US, 1915)

Blair Witch Project, The (Daniel Myrick and Eduardo Sanchez, US, 1999)

Bloc Party (Michel Gondry, US, 2006)

*Bloody Sunday (*Paul Greengrass, UK, 2002)

Blues and Twos (Carlton, 1993)

Book Group, The (Channel 4, 2002–3)

Bowling for Columbine (Michael Moore, US, 2002)

Boys Who Killed Stephen Lawrence, The (BBC, 2006)

Bubble (Steven Soderbergh, US, 2006)

Bullet Boy (Saul Dibb, UK, 2004)

Capturing the Friedmans (Andrew Jarecki, US, 2003)

Castaway (BBC1, 2000)

Cathy Come Home (Ken Loach, UK, 1966)

Chronicle of a Summer (Jean Rouch and Edgar Morin, France, 1961)

Churchill's Island (Stuart Legg, Canada, 1941)

Citizen Kane (Orson Welles, US, 1941)

City Hospital (BBC1, 1998–present)

Clampers (BBC1, 1998)

Convent, The (BBC2, 2006)

Coppers (Sky One, 1994)

Cops (Fox, 1989–present)

Corporation, The (Mark Achbar and Jennifer Abbot, Canada, 2003)

CSA: Confederate States of America (Kevin Wilmott, US, 2004)

Culloden (BBC, 1964)

Curb Your Enthusiasm (HBO, 2000–present)

Darwin's Nghtmare (Hubert Sauper, Austria/Belgium/France, 2004)

Day Britain Stopped, The (BBC, 2003)

Days of Hope (BBC, 1975)

*Deal, The (*Stephen Frears, 2004)

Death of a Princess (Granada, 1980)

Desert Victory (Roy Boulting, UK, 1943)

Don't Look Back (D A Pennebaker, US, 1967)

Dragon's Den (BBC2, 2006)

Drifters (John Grierson, UK, 1929)

Driving School (BBC, 1997)

Dying for Drugs (Channel 4, 2003)

Dying Rooms, The (Channel 4, 1995)

Elephant (Gus Van Sant, US, 2004)

Enron: The Smartest Guys in the Room (Alex Gibney, US, 2005)

Escape to the Country (BBC2, 2002–present)

Être et Avoir (Nicholas Philibert, France, 2002)

Fahrenheit 9/11 (Michael Moore, US, 2004)

Fame Academy (BBC1, 2002)

Family, The (BBC, 1974)

Fast Food Nation (Richard Linklater, US, 2006)

Festen (Thomas Vinterberg, Denmark, 1997)

Festival (Annie Griffin, UK, 2005)

Fires Were Started (Humphrey Jennings, UK, 1943)

Geri (Molly Dineen, UK, 2001)

Ghostwatch (BBC1, 1992)

Gimme Shelter (Albert and David Maysles, US, 1970)

Glastonbury (Julien Temple, UK, 2006)

Government Inspector, The (Channel 4, 2005)

Grass (Merian C Cooper and Ernest B Schoedsack, US, 1925)

Grey Gardens (Albert and David Maysles, US, 1975)

Hamburg Cell, The (Channel 4, 2004)

Harlan County, USA (Barbara Kopple, US, 1976)

High School (Fred Wiseman, US, 1968)

Honey We're Killing the Kids (BBC3, 2005–6)

Hoop Dreams (Steve James, US, 1994)

Hotel (BBC, 1997)

House of Tiny Tearaways, The (2005–present)

Housing Problems (Arthur Elton, E H Anstey, UK, 1935)

In Bed with Madonna (Alek Keshishian, US, 1991)

In the Land of the Head-Hunters (Edward S Curtis, US, 1914)

Inconvenient Truth, An (Davis Guggenheim, US, 2006)

Industrial Britain (Robert Flaherty, UK, 1931)

It Happened Here (Kevin Brownlow and Andrew Rollo, UK, 1966)

Jamie's School Dinners (Channel 4, 2005)

Jazz Singer, The (Alan Crosland, US, 1927)

Juvenile Liaison (Nick Broomfield, UK, 1975)

Kids (Larry Clark, US, 1996)

Kids behind Bars (BBC, 2005)

Kidulthood (Menaj Huda, UK, 2006)

Kurt and Courtney (Nick Broomfield, UK, 1998)

Last Broadcast, The (Stefan Avalos and Lance Weiler, US, 1998)

Life of Grime, A (BBC1, 1998–present),

*Listen to Britain (*Humphrey Jennings, UK, 1942)

Louisiana Story (Robert Flaherty, US, 1948)

Magnificent Ambersons, The (Orson Welles, US, 1942)

Man with the Movie Camera (Dziga Vertov, USSR, 1929)

March of the Penguins (Luc Jacquet, France, 2005)

Men against the Arctic (Winston Hibler, US, 1955)

Monster (Patty Jenkins, US, 2003)

Murder of Stephen Lawrence, The (Paul Greengrass, UK, 1999)

Murderball (Henry Alex Rubin and Dana Adam Shapiro, US, 2005)

Nanook of the North (Robert Flaherty, US/France, 1922)

New York Doll (Greg Whiteley, US, 2005)

Night Mail (Harry Watt and Basil Wright, UK, 1936)

Office, The (BBC, 2001–3)

*Olympia (*Leni Riefenstahl, Germany, 1935)

Open Road, The (Claude Friese-Greene, UK, 1926)

Out of Control (BBC1, 2002)

Outfoxed (Robert Greenwald, US, 2004)

Paradise Lost: The Child Murders at Robin Hood Hills (Joe Berlinger and
    Bruce Sinofsky, US, 1996)

Paris Is Burning (Jennie Livingston, US, 1990)

Primary (Robert Drew, US, 1960)

Punishment Park (Peter Watkins, UK, 1971)

Queen, The (Stephen Frears, UK/France/Italy, 2006)

Queen's Sister, The (Simon Cellan Jones, 2005)

Raging Bull (Martin Scorsese, US, 1980)

Real World, The (MTV, 1992)

Roger and Me (Michael Moore, US, 1989)

Seaside Parish, A (BBC2, 2004–present)

Salesman (Albert and David Maysles, US, 1969)

Scum (Alan Clarke, BBC, 1977)

Secret Policeman, The (BBC, 2003)

Serengeti Shall Not Die (Bernhard Grzimek, West Germany, 1959)

Shipman (ITV, 2002)

Shipyard (Paul Rotha, UK, 1935*)*

Silent World, The (Jacques-Yves Cousteau, France, 1956)

Smallpox (BBC, 2002)

Song of Ceylon, The (Basil Wright, UK, 1934)

Spellbound (Jeffrey Blitz, US, 2003)

Street Fight (Marshall Curry, US, 2005)

Super Size Me (Morgan Spurlock, US, 2004)

Supervolcano (BBC1, 2005)

Survivor (Paramount, 2000–)

Take, The (Avi Lewis, Canada, 2004)

Target for Tonight (Harry Watt, UK, 1941)

Tattooed Tears (Nick Broomfield, UK, 1978)

Taxi Driver (Martin Scorsese, US, 1976)

Temptation Island (Fox, 2001–2003)

Thin Blue Line, The (Errol Morris, US, 1989)

Times of Harvey Milk, The (Rob Epstein, US, 1984)

Titicut Follies (Frederick Wiseman, US, 1967)

Touching the Void (Kevin MacDonald, UK, 2003)

Tracking Down Maggie (Nick Broomfield, UK, 1994)

Traffic Cops (BBC1, 1998–present),

Triumph of the Will (Leni Riefenstahl, Germany, 1935)

United 93 (Paul Greengrass, US/UK/France, 2006)

Unknown White Male (Rupert Murray, US, 2006)

Vanessa (ITV, 1994)

Vet School (ITV, !993–4)

Voyage to the Congo (Marc Allégret and André Gide, Belgium, 1927)

Walmart: The High Cost of Low Price (Robert Greenwald, US, 2005)

War Game, The (Peter Watkins, 1965)

Wassup Rockers, The (Larry Clark, US, 2005)

Who Bombed Birmingham? (ITV, 1990)

Who Killed the Electric Car? (Chris Payne, US, 2006)

Why We Fight (Frank Capra, US, 1942–5)

Wisconsin Death Trip (James Marsh, US, 1999)

Workers Leaving the Factory (Louis Lumière, France, 1895)

World Trade Center (Oliver Stone, US, 2006)

World without Water, A (Channel 4, 2006)

Year at Kew, A (BBC2, 2004–present)

Useful websites

www.bbc.co.uk/bbcfour/documentaries/storyville/
Provides details of the documentaries produced in the *Storyville* series, links to useful websites, interviews with documentary-makers etc.

www.channel4.com/fourdocs/
Very detailed site including timelines, articles, interviews and documentaries to download. There is also the chance to upload your own documentary.

www.dochouse.org/
Dochouse is an organisation devoted to the development of documentary in the UK through screening and production. Website gives details of events and opportunities to get involved.

www.drewassociates.net/
Website of Richard Drew, one of the founder members of the Direct cinema movement, provides information on past and current developments in observational documentary-making.

www.griersontrust.org/index.htm
Organisation which promotes the legacy of John Grierson and recognises the work of a range of documentary-makers through their annual awards.

www.screenonline.org.uk/film/id/446186/index.html
The BFI website examines the development of the documentary in Britain and provides extracts of (often rare) documentaries.

Acknowledgements

I would like to thank the editors, Vivienne Clark and Wendy Earle, for their expert and helpful advice. I am very grateful to family, friends and colleagues who read drafts, discussed documentary with me, recommended resources and were extremely generous in lending films and books.